CAMBRIDGE LIBRARY COLLECTION

Books of enduring scholarly value

Travel and Exploration

The history of travel writing dates back to the Bible, Caesar, the Vikings and the Crusaders, and its many themes include war, trade, science and recreation. Explorers from Columbus to Cook charted lands not previously visited by Western travellers, and were followed by merchants, missionaries, and colonists, who wrote accounts of their experiences. The development of steam power in the nineteenth century provided opportunities for increasing numbers of 'ordinary' people to travel further, more economically, and more safely, and resulted in great enthusiasm for travel writing among the reading public. Works included in this series range from first-hand descriptions of previously unrecorded places, to literary accounts of the strange habits of foreigners, to examples of the burgeoning numbers of guidebooks produced to satisfy the needs of a new kind of traveller - the tourist.

Notes of a Journey from Hankow to Ta-li Fu

The journal of Augustus Raymond Margary's groundbreaking journey from Hankow in the Hubei province of central China, to Bhamo in Upper Burma was published in 1875, soon after his death. Margary was part of the Chinese consular service and had lived in China since 1867, working as an interpreter. This journal begins in August 1874 at the start of his journey, the purpose of which was to meet Colonel Horace Browne to act as his interpreter as he attempted to open a overland trade route between China and India. Margary was the first Englishman successfully to complete the 1,800 mile trip through Szechwan to Yunnan, doing so in six months. On the return trip, he and two servants made a diversion, hearing of danger on his proposed route, but were murdered in the town of Manwyne, leading to public outrage and commemorative publication of accounts of his life and travels.

Cambridge University Press has long been a pioneer in the reissuing of out-of-print titles from its own backlist, producing digital reprints of books that are still sought after by scholars and students but could not be reprinted economically using traditional technology. The Cambridge Library Collection extends this activity to a wider range of books which are still of importance to researchers and professionals, either for the source material they contain, or as landmarks in the history of their academic discipline.

Drawing from the world-renowned collections in the Cambridge University Library, and guided by the advice of experts in each subject area, Cambridge University Press is using state-of-the-art scanning machines in its own Printing House to capture the content of each book selected for inclusion. The files are processed to give a consistently clear, crisp image, and the books finished to the high quality standard for which the Press is recognised around the world. The latest print-on-demand technology ensures that the books will remain available indefinitely, and that orders for single or multiple copies can quickly be supplied.

The Cambridge Library Collection will bring back to life books of enduring scholarly value (including out-of-copyright works originally issued by other publishers) across a wide range of disciplines in the humanities and social sciences and in science and technology.

Notes of
a Journey from
Hankow to Ta-li Fu

AUGUSTUS RAYMOND MARGARY

CAMBRIDGE UNIVERSITY PRESS

Cambridge, New York, Melbourne, Madrid, Cape Town, Singapore,
São Paolo, Delhi, Dubai, Tokyo

Published in the United States of America by Cambridge University Press, New York

www.cambridge.org
Information on this title: www.cambridge.org/9781108015196

© in this compilation Cambridge University Press 2010

This edition first published 1875
This digitally printed version 2010

ISBN 978-1-108-01519-6 Paperback

NOTES

OF A

JOURNEY

FROM

HANKOW TO TA-LI FU,

BY THE LATE

AUGUSTUS RAYMOND MARGARY,

CHINA CONSULAR SERVICE.

———◆———

SHANGHAI:

PRINTED BY F. & C. WALSH, No. 3, CANTON ROAD.

——

1875.

The Government of India having signified a desire to send a small Mission into Yün Nan, a passport was obtained last summer by the British Legation from the Chinese Government, to enable four officers and gentlemen, with their followers, to cross the frontier from the Burmese side. Mr. MARGARY, a young member of the China Consular Service, of great promise, was sent with a separate passport to meet the above Mission, which had been placed under the leadership of Colonel HORACE BROWNE. Having joined Colonel BROWNE at Bhamo, the Mission had entered China, and was but a short distance from Manwyne, when Mr. MARGARY pushed on to that town. He had passed a week in it on his journey southward. At Manwyne, according to testimony too strong to be doubted, he was murdered on the 21st February. An attack was made on the following morning on Colonel BROWNE'S' party, which, however, after a sharp struggle, was enabled to draw off without serious loss.

Mr. MARGARY in compliance with his instructions kept a journal, and the portion of it which records his experiences as far as Ta-li Fu has happily been saved. There are various gaps in it, to be explained probably by the fact that he suffered from time to time seriously in health. The remainder was too probably with him when he was murdered.

Believing that, their interest on other grounds apart, Mr. MARGARY's notes will be regarded as an acceptable souvenir by the many who knew his merits and lament his cruel fate, Her Majesty's Minister has sanctioned their publication.

For completeness sake, an Itinerary has been appended to the journal.

ITINERARY.

DATE & HOUR OF ARRIVAL.		PLACE.	DISTANCE (IN LI) FROM PREVIOUS PLACE.
Sept.		Hankow :—	
4	3.30 P.M.	武昌 Wu-ch'ang	20
5	2 P.M.	金口 Chin-k'ou	——
,,	Evening	冬瓜腦 Tung-kua-nao......	105 (from Wu-ch'ang.)
6	——	簰洲 P'ai Chou..........	45
7	12.30	小划攏 Hsiao-hua-pai	45
8	Evening	胡心洲 Hu-hsin Chou	60
9	Evening	六溪口 Lu-ch'i-k'ou	60
11	——	新堤 Hsin-t'i.............	60
,,	Evening	螺山 Lo-shan	45
......	....	....	......
20	Evening	君山 Chün-shan..........	——
21	Evening	—— Nan-chai............	180
22	——	—— Ni-hsin-t'ang	60
,,	Evening	Yin-ho Hsiang	40
23	11 A.M.	龍陽縣 Lung-yang Hsien	——
,,	3.30 P.M.	—— Liao-ya-tsui........	70 from Yin-ho Hsiang.
24	6 P.M.	—— Shih-ma P'u........	40
25	Evening	常德府 Ch'ang-tê Fu......	20
27	3 P.M.	—— Ta-ch'i-k'ou........	20
28	2 P.M.	桃源縣 T'ao-yuen Hsien...	70
,,	——	白馬渡 Pai-ma Tu..........	20
,,	Evening	—— Shui-ch'i............	5
29	Evening	—— (Small village.)	——
30	Evening	—— (Small village.)	——

Date & Hour of arrival.		Place.		Distance (in li) from previous Place.
Oct.				
1	———	———	———	
2	———	———	———	35
3	7 P.M.	府州辰	Ch'ên-chou Fu....	70
4	———	溪瀘	Lu-ch'i	———
5	5 P.M.	———	Pu-shih............	———
6	7 A.M.	縣谿辰	Ch'ên-chi Hsien...	———
......	....			....
27	5 P.M.	府遠鎮	Chên-yuen Fu.....	———
28	———	———		
29	———	縣秉施	Shih-ping Hsien...	12
„	Evening	———	———	———
30	———	———	Hsin-chou..........	30
31	Evening	洞風大	Ta-fêng-tung	———
Nov.				
1	10 A.M.	縣平清	Ch'ing-p'ing Hsien	———
2	———			
3	———	縣定貴	Kuei-ting Hsien...	45
4	6 P.M.	縣里龍	Lung-li Hsien	75
5	———	府陽貴	Kuei-yang Fu	———
8	———	縣鎮清	Ch'ing-chên Hsien	69
9	———	縣溪清	Ch'ing-ch'i Hsien.	62
10	6 P.M.	府順安	An-shun Fu	80
11	———	州寗鎮	Chên-ning Chou...	60
„	———	———	Huang-kuo-su	25
12	———	———	———	50
13	———	廳岱郎	Lang-tai T'ing	60
14	———	———	Mê-k'ou............	Short stage.

Date & Hour of arrival.			Place.	Distance (in li) from previous Place.
Nov. 15	——	——	Hua-king	35
16	——	——	——	——
17	——	——	Yang-shun	——
18	——	廳安普	P'u-an T'ing	40
19	——		——	——
20	——	縣彝平	P'ing-i Hsien	——
21	——	白水	Pai-shui	——
22	——		Hai-tzŭ P'u	Half way to Chan-i Chou.
,,	——	州益霑	Chan-i Chou	——
23	——	州龍馬	Ma-lung Chou......	——
24	——	——	Pai-tzŭ P'u	40
,,	——	司隆易	I-lung Ssu	40
25	——	林楊	Yang-lin.............	75
26	——	橋板	Pan-ch'iao	——
27	Noon	府南雲	Yun-nan Fu.........	105 from Yang-lin.
......	....	....	....	....
Dec. 2	——	口鷄碧	Pi-chi K'ou.........	35
3	——	州甯安	An-ning Chou......	40
4	——	關鵶老	Lao-ya Kuan.......	70
5	——	縣豐祿	Lu-fêng Hsien......	75
6	——	資捨	Shê-tzŭ	90

Date & Hour of arrival.		Place.	Distance (in li) from previous Place.
Dec. 7	—— 縣通廣	Kuang-t'ung Hsien	——
8	—— 站腰	Yao-chan............	——
,,	—— 府雄楚	Ch'u-hsiung Fu....	——
9	—— 州南鎮	Chên-nan Chou....	95
10	—— ——	Sha-ch'iao..........	35
11	—— ——	Lien-p'êng..........	95

Four more stages to Ta-li Fu.

JOURNAL.

HAVING received orders, while at Shanghai, to hold myself in readiness to proceed to Yunnan at a short notice, I set myself without delay to make such preparations as would enable me to start with dispatch, yet at the same time without definitely incurring an outlay in case of a countermand. The above intimation was received through Mr. Medhurst, on the 9th August, and on 15th and the 21st, I had the honour to receive full and confidential instructions from H. B. M. Minister, which directed me to start at once, and accordingly I left Shanghai on the night of Saturday 22nd for Hankow. Arrived at Kiukiang on the 25th, I remained at that port two days to consult with Mr. Vice-Consul King about the route, as directed in my instructions. This officer had recently ascended the Yangtsze to Chung-ching, and very readily gave me the benefit of his valuable observations, besides furnishing me with books and papers on the subject, including his own private diary of the trip.

August 28th, 1874.—Reached Hankow in exceptionally hot weather, and unfortunately in a very bad state of health, which continued for several days and retarded my final preparations. Mr. Consul Hughes had called upon the Viceroy with the letter from the Tsungli Yamen, and found H.E. had already received despatches from Peking on the subject of my trip. The Viceroy in conversation strongly recommended the Hu Nan and Kwei Chou route as that which was usually followed by officials, and was just now selected by the Governor of Yun Nan, who was on his way thither. Acting on this advice, and moreover finding that time and expense were likely to be saved by adopting this road, I decided to do so with Mr. Hughes's full concurrence. The Viceroy was informed on the 31st of this decision, and wrote to say that he had forthwith directed all the officials along the route to aid and protect my progress.

The 31st, 1st and 2nd were taken up in bargaining for and procuring a boat, hiring servants, and concluding financial arrangements, which at first threatened to become exceedingly troublesome. But an order was at length obtained on a Shen Si branch bank which had been set up in Yun Nan very recently, and which was indeed an encouraging sign of returning order and prosperity in that long-disturbed province. The banker who supplied me with this order had the civility to call, and proved to be a man of great consequence and ability. He informed me that the Government of Yun Nan was also supplied with funds through his bank. Along with the order a tally weight of brass was given to me, which was to be presented at the bank in Yun-nan Fu to serve as the standard of payment. And four per cent discount was the rate charged for the accommodation.

My preparations were completed for starting on the 3rd, but unfortunately an attack of illness obliged me to put off the departure till next day. The boat was one of those commonly called a mandarin boat, long and narrow, and divided into five or six compartments which ran the whole length of the craft, the centre being occupied with a somewhat wider and neater space, fitted with chairs and tables and suited for the reception of guests. Each compartment contained a couple of low berths, one on each side of the passage running down the middle. But as a Chinaman's average stature falls far short of an Englishman's proportions, I found it necessary to lengthen the bedside of my compartment by removing the dividing panel. A similar precaution had to be taken with regard to the floor, whereof the boards were lowered fully six inches to save my head from the pains and penalties of trying to unroof the not too substantial top. A regular Chinese form of agreement was drawn up by the boat-owner and handed over to me. The main conditions were that he should convey me to Chen-yuan Fu in Kwei Chou for the sum of 110,000 cash, which was to be paid in several instalments at different places on the way, starting with a prepayment of 60,000 cash at Hankow. This sum was to include everything and to free me from all those incidental appeals on behalf of the crew which so frequently spring up *en route* to delay and annoy the traveller. My party consisted of five, comprising a writer, an official messenger, a cook, and my body servant. With regard to the necessary supplies for daily expenses between Hankow and Yun-nan Fu, where alone I had credit for funds, I should mention that I adopted the following plan which appeared to be the best that any one could suggest. It was to take with me in the boat a quantity of cash sufficient to cover everything as far as Chen-yuan Fu, and to leave a margin wherewith to pay the first instalment for chairs in the land journey, which would commence at that place. In addition to this I procured a hundred taels worth of small silver ingots, weighing five taels each, which formed a very convenient parcel, and one easily concealed in a box of winter clothes reserved for Yun Nan. These small ingots are called at Hankow *chin sha yin*. The cash was entrusted to my official messenger, whose receipt for the amount relieved my mind of the monstrous anxiety of having to watch over the safety of what seemed a vast hoard when converted into the bulky proportions of copper currency. The whole mass was deposited loosely in strings of a 1,000 cash (called a *tiao*) on the floor of the boat, beneath the servant's couch, and there it might remain without the smallest fear of theft, although within easy reach of a pilfering arm. The Chinese are no thieves. Their purloinings take a different form, which I might charitably term "commission," but prefer to stigmatize a "squeeze."

September 4th.—Left Hankow at 11 A.M., crossed the river and tracked along under the walls of Wu-ch'ang. Made little progress against the strong current, without the aid of a breath of wind. At 3.30 brought up in a creek facing the southern suburb of the capital, having progressed but 20 li. Boatmen expected a storm from the northwest, and declined to proceed. Numbers of junks large and small were running in for shelter. I landed and took a short stroll with my writer, without exciting any incivility, though a good deal of curiosity. Finding my boat jambed in among a myriad of small craft, and deprived of every avenue by which a breeze might be wafted in to cool an atmosphere heated up to 92° throughout the day, I compelled the boatmen to retrace our course to the mouth of the creek, where shortly after we found ourselves in a perfect babel of tongues, aroused by the fast-approaching wind and thunderstorm. The men began to reproach me for bringing our small boat into such dangerous proximity to larger craft, and for some time, as the wind freshened and the vast flotilla began to swing about in constant collision, the uproar of voices surpassed all description. No harm was done however, for the storm passed off as suddenly as it came, and left us refreshed by a cooler temperature.

September 5th.—Started with a fair wind, and completed 105 li. Passed Ching-k'ou at 2 P.M. I was down with fever during the morning, but succeeded in walking along the towing path for some distance during the afternoon. The temperature had been reduced ten degrees by the storm. Country appeared to be low and subject to inundation. A few fields of cotton in the very poorest condition, and large quantities of sesamum which seemed healthy, were the only products of cultivation. A pretty view of hills to the north opened out from time to time. On the north bank of the river, *kaoliang* or *sorghum* was cultivated, as well as small quantities of indigo. Reached Tung-kua-nao [a Lekin Station, and anchorage for junks], in the evening, and remained there for the night. A messenger from Hankow arrived at 9 P.M. with a telegram from Calcutta, forwarded by Mr. Medhurst, to the following effect:—

"Calcutta, 31st August, 1874. To Consul Medhurst, Shanghai.
"Interpreter had better join party at Rangoon by sea. I am telegraphing to Mr. Wade. Interpreter had better postpone departure pending further orders from Pekin."—"Foreign."

In the absence of further instructions, and not being pressed for time by this route, I wrote back to say that I should proceed leisurely on, to a place called Lo-shan, and there wait for further orders. My reasons for taking this course were strengthened by a desire to save time. In the first place the current of the Yangtsze being exceedingly strong, it was better to halt as near the Tungting Lake as possible, so

4

that in case of receiving orders to proceed, I could push on faster. In the next place I calculated that the time required for an answer to arrive would only necessitate a delay of four or five days at Lo-shan. Yao-chou Fu at the entrance of the lake had so often evinced an active hostility to foreigners that I preferred a more comfortable halting place, and selected Lo-shan, which was 80 li short of the former city.

September 6th.—Tracked against a south wind all day. Country flat and dry, cultivated with cotton and sesamum. Only made 45 li, and anchored at P'ai-chou in company with numbers of river junks. Left the boat and walked across a bend to the village of P'ai-chou, which looked exceedingly pretty, embowered in masses of trees. On a nearer view the village expanded into a large straggling town, full of well built substantial houses, which spoke of considerable prosperity. My writer and messenger were with me. We met with civility at first, and sat down at one house chatting with the host. But as we passed the quarter by the junks the wildest excitement broke out. A mob collected and followed me for fully half a mile along the bund until I found my boat. It was not very exhilarating, and I confess I failed to enjoy the fun as much as the rest, for they shouted and screamed with laughter, dancing round me as if they were intensely amused. P'ai-chou lies on the right bank of the river.

September 7th.—Only moved on 45 li to a place called Hsiao-hua-pai, where we arrived at 12.30, and found it intolerably hot. This place was merely a convenient anchorage for junks, owing to the existence of a creek. The few shops which formed a village were only there for the benefit of the junks; like the Lekin barrier, which was there no doubt with the same benevolent object.

September 8th.—Got over 60 li to Hu-hsin Chou, an island in the big river, separated from the mainland by a narrow channel, which afforded a good anchorage to boats passing up. The district city of Chia-yü Hsien was only removed a few li from this spot, and appeared to be well placed among low hills and a quantity of trees. The island itself was thickly covered with sand hidden by luxuriant growth of a grassy weed, which deceived the eye at a short distance with the appearance of a meadow. The heat was very great all day.

September 9th.—Tracked all day against wind and stream. Arriving among the hills. Stopped at Lu-ch'i-k'ou, 60 li from the last stage. Here a clear mountain river flowed down from the Tea hills and went to pollute itself in the muddy bosom of the Yangtsze. I was enabled to have a plunge and swim, morning and evening, in this comparatively clear stream. Lu-ch'i-k'ou, which by the way took its name from the river, was a gunboat station. A large man-of-war junk moored close to shore was used as a depôt hulk, and dwelling for the officer in command. Several river gunboats lay alongside. The commander of the station, who held the rank of *yu-chi* (a blue buttoned officer) had a residence on shore. Twenty-one gunboats scattered up and down the river received their orders from his hands.

September 10th.—Remained all day at Lu-ch'i-k'ou, wind bound. Met with occasional rudeness while taking walks on shore, not from any grown up persons, but from boys, who repeatedly shouted out " Foreign Devil," from a safe distance. The night watches were struck on board the naval hulk with the usual measured strokes of a drum, and these again were subdivided into periods of 20 minutes by similar strokes of a triangle. Each new watch was ushered in by a prolonged flourish on the drum, which broke my slumbers unpleasantly.

September 11th.—A strong favouring breeze having set in from the north, we sprang along under sail in company with a large fleet of river traders, and reached Hsin T'i, a distance of 60 li, in fairly quick time. Hsin T'i appeared to be a flourishing place, and a great number of river craft was massed in the open unsheltered anchorage which faced the long straight frontage of the town. After stopping but a short time at this place, the boatmen, feeling insecure in such an exposed position, again set sail and ran on 45 li to Lo-shan, the place I had fixed for awaiting further orders at. Hsin T'i was governed by a *chou-t'ung.* A *tao-t'ai* was also established on the bank of the river whose sole duty it was to collect the timber dues from the rafts, which float down in large numbers. These rafts present a very curious appearance. Seen from a short distance they look like a floating village with a brisk population, and on a nearer view one cannot help admiring the ingenious construction. The larger lengths of timber are closely massed together forming a compact raft of no mean dimensions, down the centre of which are constructed a series of neat huts for the crew to live in. The head of the raft is shaped off to somewhat of a sharp prow, and at the stern a gallery runs out fitted with steering apparatus. The fast stream of the Yangtsze carries them down with sufficient speed, but they are also furnished with enormous sweeps requiring the strength of ten or twelve men to manipulate. The raftsmen appear to possess a magnificent form. I have nowhere seen such fine athletic frames in China, and could not help stopping to admire the splendid development of muscle, which was so well displayed as they swayed to and fro with the enormous sweeps. Three or four of these rafts generally came down in company, one behind the other in a long string, and for means of communication a diminutive raft, rowed by five men, answered every purpose of a boat. It had all the appearance of a long legged fly shooting across the water in spasmodic spurts. It may be worthy of remark that I noticed, first at P'ai-chou, and repeatedly afterwards at other places further up the river, the use of a cart in agriculture. It is not often that one sees a Chinese farmer make use of anything so handy. But in this instance the form of the vehicle was so novel and so different to that which is sometimes used in the Province of Chih Li that it deserves to be described. The diversity of shape is itself a striking fact, in a country where similar operations are carried on in precisely the same way and with the same implements in provinces far apart and disconnected by dialect. The main difference lay in the fact that whereas the northern carts, like others all the world over, are built with their wheels outside the body of the vehicle, the centre of gravity of which is placed low down, these Hu Pei carts enclose their wheels, and are consequently raised high above them, like a railway carriage. The cart simply amounts to a wide platform poised above two wheels upon the stout axles which protrude. Dragged along by the water buffalo, of all beasts the most ungainly, its appearance is more quaint than elegant.

September 12th.—In view of having to pass several days at Lo-shan I deemed it prudent to call on the local official, although he had neither position nor authority of any consequence whatever. Of military grade, which is looked down upon in China, and of no higher rank than a *pa-tsung*, or ensign, his position in the place at the head of only eighteen men was nothing more than that of a head policeman. Lo-shan contains something over a thousand families, and its civil government, like that of many similar growing places in the district, lies in the jurisdiction of the magistrate who presides over the head city, ten miles away. Having announced my intention of calling at 4 P. M., I waited through a very hot day for the welcome diversion. But I was little prepared for the hubbub my presence was going to create. Lo-shan had never been feasted with even the sight of a foreigner, and their very ignorance of his conformation put a boldness to the curiosity of the mob which surrounded me with shouts and abusive language as I proceeded in a hired chair, the meanest of its kind, to the poor abode of the local official. As is usually the case in China, the rabble burst into the courtyard of the Yamen, and were with difficulty repressed from filling even the audience room, by the whips of the lictors at the door, who plied their arms with a will. An interview is never private in China, any more than correspondence. It is not considered indecorous to take up any written decument, whether intended to be confidential or not, and to read it calmly through. I have seen a Mandarin, while making a call on the Consul, step up to the writer's table and coolly putting on his spectacles, read a letter which had just been prepared for another official on an important subject. So, too, every interview I have had the honour to assist at, has been swelled by the presence of a number of idle spectators, from Yamen runners down to the household servants of the Mandarin. I found the official in question to be a very civil and obliging man, well informed and well disposed towards foreigners. He was reading a book written by a Chinaman of rank, named Pin, who some years ago had been sent to Europe to record his impressions of foreign countries, and subsequently published the volume referred to,. Calling my attention to the book he frequently remarked that England must be a fine country. On taking leave I complained of the conduct of the people, and the officer immediately ordered a couple of his men to escort me back, but their efforts were barely equal to repressing the excited crowd which followed us to the boat and stood in a dense mass round my chair. The best way of pacifying a Chinese mob is by talking to them and showing them at once that you are familiar with their language and literature. Accordingly I addressed a few words to my aggressive audience, which had the almost immediate effect of quieting and dispersing it. The disturbance was mainly owing to the presence of a large number of young soldiers who were on their way to the seat of impending war in Formosa, and also to the fact of its being a sort of public holiday, for strolling players had arrived and set up a *sing-song* which attracted spectators from all the country round.

September 13th to 19th.—All this time was unfortunately lost in waiting for further orders with respect to the last telegram from Calcutta. But as no messenger had yet made his appearance, and ample time had passed for letters to have reached me, I resolved to proceed on the 20th. No other course was open to me. Further delay would have made it too late to follow the overland route, and it could only have been abandoned at a considerable cost. Lo-shan proved to be an exceedingly pleasant place to stop at. A stretch of downs surrounded the town and afforded me both exercise and sport. I was able to take many a walk free from intruders, and by permission of the Mandarin, I shot over some excellent cover. Immediately behind these downs extended a flat plain, as far as the eye could reach, cultivated with rice, and the lotus. This is a great lotus district, and a very curious special industry has grown out of it for the people of Lo-shan. It appears that the art or knack of extracting the kernel of the lotus nut from its hard shell is only properly understood at this place, and the produce of the whole district is sent to Lo-shan, whence it is distributed in its edible form up and down the river. The view across the river, which was here fully a mile and a half wide, * *

September 20th.—Still no messenger. Started at 11 A.M. with a strong breeze from the north-east, which accelerated our progress, but struck me down with fever. Splendid views of green country and mountains in the background extended the whole way along the right bank to Yao-chou Fu. We were stopped by a Leking Barrier which was stationed at a distance of 20 to 30 li from Yao-chou Fu. I immediately sent my card to the official in charge, but in the meanwhile, much to my annoyance, I found a soldier poking about among my boxes with a long javelin. A few words made him desist at once and leave the boat. We then sailed for the celebrated island of Chün-shan, which lies at the entrance of the lake opposite the city of Yao-chou, and some thirty li away from the latter. Here we took leave of the muddy Yangtsze, and entered into cleaner waters of a pale green hue. The panorama of Yao-chou Fu and the surrounding hills, as seen from the island of Chün-shan, is certainly very striking, and the city is placed on a beautiful site. The red sand-stone, which seems to be the prevailing formation, crops out in various places, adding richness and colour to the scene. Yao-chou Fu used to be the place of transhipment for the grain tribute of Hu Nan, and in those days of prosperity, the business of the place was very large, and the wharves crowded with junks, but since the tax has been levied in coin, all this activity has vanished from the place.

September 21st.—The island of Chün-shan is celebrated for producing the finest tea in China. A yearly supply of 40 catties is required for the Emperor's use, and about 160 catties more are annually appropriated by all the high officials of the Province from the Viceroy downwards. The Taiping rebels deliberately destroyed a great number of the shrubs, so that the proprietors have but a small crop to dispose of. The price in former days was as high as $5 a catty. The wind continuing favourable and strong, my boatman took the unusual course of sailing straight across the lake instead of creeping along the shore. We actually accomplished 180 li at one stretch, and entered the river at 9 P.M. The lake is extremely shallow, and seems to be very little used, for I only saw one or two junks during the day. Unfortunately I was feeling very ill all day with fever. A perfect plague of flies infested us the whole way from Chün-shan to the other end of the lake. These flies were armed with a strong proboscis with which they could inflict a sting quite as acute as that of a mosquito, though free from venom. Neither pain nor mark remained on brushing away the insect. The Chinese have a legend that they are the soldiers of the Lake Spirit, who sends them to attack all intruders of his domain. We anchored at a place called Nan-chai.

September 22nd.—Started at 6 A.M. and sailed up the Yuan River with a good breeze until we arrived at a considerable town stretching along the face of the river, called Ni Hsin T'ang, 60 li from the mouth. After remaining half an hour to procure provisions we proceeded on our way. The army of the Lake Spirit here left us as suddenly as it had come. The scenery of the river is exceedingly pretty. In lieu of bare towing paths and muddy deposits, which invariably meet the eye in many parts of China, here I was delighted to find grassy banks covered thickly with willow trees. I landed and walked as far as my weak state permitted. Everywhere the signs of prosperity abounded. There was neat and careful cultivation of cotton. The homesteads adjoining the little farms were well built and well provided, and men, women and children seemed to be happy and thriving. I met with civility from all. Stopped for the night at Yin Ho Hsiang, having run over a hundred li from our last halt.

September 23rd.—Started at 5 A.M. and progressed slowly. The weather began to change and fall in temperature. Passed Lung-yang Hsien, at a distance, by 11 A.M. I felt very unwell. At 3.30 P.M., rain prevented further progress, and we stopped at Liao Ya Tsui, only 70 li in advance.

September 24th.—Continued to rain all the morning, and the most miserable weather lasted all day. In the afternoon, however, a slight improvement induced the boatmen to track on till 6 P.M., when we stopped at Shih-ma P'u, 20 li from Ch'ang-tê. We had only progressed 40 li. About midway we came across a small tributary river, which does not appear in three several maps which I possess. I am told, however, by the boatmen that this river communicates with Sha-shih, on the Yang-tsze, and also with Tseng-shih and Li-chou. I had remarked on my way up that there were very few boats on the river, but this tributary fully accounted for it, according to the statements of my informants. They say that half the trade of Ch'ang-tê passes up northwards to the great marts I have mentioned, through this connecting stream.

September 25th.—Reached Ch'ang-tê, and had a fine view of the city as we passed along its face on the opposite side of the river. The wall of the city, as I observed after we had crossed over, was built very close to the river side, leaving no room whatever for an open suburb to spring up outside, which was absolutely necessary for the carrying on of trade. The difficulty, here, has been got over by building wooden tenements on long piles, embedded in the very mud of the sloping bank. The result is an exceedingly odd appearance of houses walking on long crocked legs and leaning at all angles.

They continue only where the wall exists, or for about a distance of three li, but the line of houses more substantially built, extends along 10 li of river frontage, and from first to last are to be seen a host of small junks anchored below, awaiting their cargo. We crossed over to the city, and I sent my card to the Prefect. I had scarcely dismissed the messenger before a boat come alongside, and a Mandarin wearing a red button, stepped into my boat. Not being prepared to receive him I hastily retired to rearrange my dress, but my visitor insisted on my making no change, shook hands with me, and said that the Prefect had especially deputed him to attend upon me, and that he should accompany me to the next Prefecture. He stayed upwards of an hour and talked incessantly. After he left, I was somewhat annoyed by people coming down to stare. In some cases they would step on the side of the boat to look in through the windows. It was the great full moon holiday, and a number of idle characters were about. No direct rudeness was offered, however, although the crowd showed itself inclined to be "larky."

September 27th.—Left Ch'ang-tê accompanied by Li Pi-shêng at 11 A.M. The weather was cloudy and the atmosphere damp. At 3 P.M. the boat was brought up at a place called Ta-ch'i-k'ou, only 20 li from Ch'ang-tê. I imagined that the weather was the cause of stopping further progress, but I was informed later, much to my dissatisfaction, that the newly hired men had to feast and drink before commencing the voyage; else they would not work happily. So that I had to submit to the delay on account of their devotion to all the customs of their class.

September 28th.—Started at daylight and by 2 o'clock reached T'ao-yuen Hsien, which is a large and flourishing city. Strange to say it possesses no walls and, I am told never had any. It is the only instance I know of a magisterial city without walls, though my writer says there are a few more. I exchanged cards with the Magistrate and proceeded as fast as we could on my way. The whole frontage of the town was stored up with earthenware water-jars and glazed flower-pots. The place was a depôt for the pottery trade, and large quantities of the above ware was passed on from T'ao-yuen Hsien to Ch'ên-chou Fu, and even on to Ch'ên-yuen Fu in Kwei Chou. It is said that the magistrate who rules over T'ao-yuen Hsien has no easy task to perform. It is the most lawless, independent district in the whole province. The people if roused by a sense of injustice or misrule won't hesitate to carry off their Chief Magistrate bodily to the Governor's capital and demand a change. Proceeded on our way 20 li to a place called Pai-ma Tu, where there is a ferry across to the right bank of the river. From that point a high road runs up to Kwei Chou, and continues on to Yun Nan. A very large trade is carried on with those provinces by this road. It is a considerably shorter route than the river, which bends about in all directions. Since this morning we have been entering mountain scenery of a very beautiful and attractive kind. Everywhere vegetation seemed to spring up in abundance. Trees multiplied, but I could not distinguish many varieties. Pines covered all the hill tops, and several stout trees of the ash kind seemed to exist below. I even came across two palms. We stopped for the night 5 li further on, at Shui-ch'i, 95 li.

September 29th.—Started 5 A.M. Li-pi-shêng, the Mandarin who has accompanied me from Ch'ang-tê, often pays me a visit and talks on any subject. I have found him an exceedingly agreeable companion. This afternoon, being anxious to take a short stroll, I went on shore, and Mr. Li readily accompanied me. The boatmen, however, tracked on in hot haste to a point much farther than I was quite able to accomplish after my long continued weakness and indisposition. We followed a beautiful path high up the green cliff, which often wound inland for a short distance, and thus added to the length of my harassing walk. Li, with great consideration, insisted on my resting often, and in many ways showed a kindness unusual in a Chinaman and an official. In the course of repeated conversations with this man, I had learnt the history of his career, and he was at no pains to conceal from me the discontent he felt at his present lot. One of Li Hung-ch'ang's right hand men in the wars of the rebellion, he had been successively rewarded with a number of lucrative posts by that powerful chief, whose confidence he still boasts of possessing. In 1864 he had an appointment at Shanghai where he acquired a liking for Europeans, which appears to have remained unimpaired. Li Hung-ch'ang continued to promote his favourite until, with a red button of the 2nd degree, and the rank of Tsungping or general, he sent him to an important post in Kwei Chou. Here, however, the little man fell ill, and was obliged to obtain leave of absence to his native city Ch'ang-tê. Since then his woes commenced. Whether it was that the Government were jealous of Li Hung-ch'ang's power, and noticing with dread the caution with which that able commander was filling important posts all over the country with his own men, had set to work to thwart him; or whether it was a *bonâ fide* compliment to Li Pi-shêng's abilities, as they would have him believe, certain it is that, so soon as he became convalescent my friend received orders from the Viceroy of Hu Kwang at Wu-ch'ang Fu, to remain at Ch'ang-tê under the orders of the *chih-fu* (prefect), as his energy and influence were required in his native district. Thus it came about that I was honoured with the company of a man of distinction, whose actual services and decoration of the red button put him somewhat above the position of the local Prefect whose orders he had to obey. Of course he was intriguing to get free, and trusted very much in my being able to give him a helping hand by reporting his diligent attention and civility to me, in my letter to H.B.M. Minister at Peking, who he hoped would incidentally mention him in terms of praise to his patron Li Hung-ch'ang. Since this morning we entered upon a complete change of scenery. The river, with its beautifully clear water, was considerably narrowed, and began to wind in and out between fine rocky gorges. The hills were tossed about in strange profusion, yet in something like symmetry of form. They were all conical and of moderate size, not exceeding 200 feet in height. But the general effect was very grand. It gave me the idea of an encampment of hills. Further on, where the gorge became wilder and the hills approached the river, I was enabled to determine the nature of the composing rock, although, without the possibility of approaching near enough to examine closely the towering cliff, I must speak with hesitation as to the correctness of my conclusions. Isolated here and there along the banks, the very heart and centre of these conical hills was laid bare to view. Cut completely in half from apex to base, as though by some mighty convulsion of nature, the hill still preserved its rounded form on the land side, covered with verdure, while to the river it presented a denuded face of grey sandstone cliff. The rocks rose perpendicularly in a triangular shape out of the shallow waters at their base, with a grandeur, which was most impressive. The whole of Hu Nan is an exceedingly good field for geological examination. Nature seems to have run riot in this region at some period in the mysterious past.

Lieut. Garnier in his excellent pamphlet describing his trip from Hankow down part of this river and up to the Yangtsze at Fuchou, describes the rivers which disappear and reappear after a subterranean course, and the many evidences of mighty convulsions of nature which met his view

The bed of this river itself and the adjoining banks offer a rich harvest to a scientific explorer. Almost every variety of strata crops out at different points. On arriving at our resting place for the night, I was very much surprised to see a small boat of the very commonest class come alongside, and a couple of disreputable looking rascals emerge from it with the card of the T'ao-yuan Magistrate in their hands. He had sent them to escort and protect !! me as far as the next Magisterial city. The Viceroy's orders were imperative, but the worthy Magistrate evaded them as far as he dared. Nothing is done thoroughly in China; the Mandarins look to their tenure of office as the golden opportunity for feathering their nests. So our worthy friend carried out his instructions as cheaply and nastily as hé was able, on this occasion. He despatched a couple of dirty scullions or some other such menials, out of the needy crowd that infests all Yameṇs, hoping no doubt that fine words and the foreigner's ignorance would hide his mean devices. The village we stopped at for the night had a special industry which occupied every family of its inhabitants. Above this point the rapids commenced, and the bamboo ropes, (of the thickness of a man's forefinger) required for tracking boats through them, were manufactured and procured at this place.

September 30th.—Li Pi-shêng left me to-day at 2.30 P.M. and returned on his homeward voyage, no doubt with a happy sense of relief from the monotonous duty of escorting a foreigner. He must have felt the ennui of toiling after my boat very keenly, for in the first place he did little else all the day but smoke opium ; and, secondly, it was his duty to accompany me to the next Prefectural city, instead of which he bid me good-bye at the boundary of the district, which oddly enough coincided with the first set of rapids we had to encounter. I was now left for " safe conduct and protection," to the care of the two miserable menials in their ridiculous boat, whose frantic efforts to keep pace with us afforded me much amusement. The sail was a marvel. Every square foot of it had a hole big enough to pass the head through, and whatever cloth remained to catch the wind had no more consistency than very old muslin.

At about 3 P.M. we passed through several rapids in succession. There was nothing formidable about them. Five men tracked along the shore, and the remainder staved the boat off sunken rocks with their bamboo poles. The scenery was wildly beautiful, and more compact than that we passed through yesterday ; a continuation of perpendicular cliffs now and then lined the river side. A mountain path, which was the highway for foot passengers, passed in some places along the very face of the upright cliff. But I noticed a heavy iron-chain cable hung in festoons, from niches cut in the rock, along the face of this dangerous path. It was the gift of a philanthropic widow, whose charity may have been evoked by the loss of a relative on the fatal spot.

October 1st.—The weather during the last ten days has been most unfavourable and unhealthy, fully bearing out part of the statement which Li Pi-shêng made at Ch'ang-tê Fu, in the course of our conversation, that the two dangerous mouths in Hu Nan were the 2nd and the 8th. I have not had a chance of recovering health and strength, and the frequent attacks of fever and diarrhœa have reduced me to a state of emaciation almost and extreme weakness. My boatmen too are attacked with simultaneous vomiting and diarrhœa accompanied with violent pains in the stomach. I cured the head boatman who suffered most, with an opium pill, the others fortunately recovering quick, or my slender store of drugs might have been exhausted in one night.

To-day we passed through the most dangerous set of rapids on the river. They extend over 30 li and are divided into three portions of ten li each by the boatmen, who name them the upper, the middle and the lower. In these rapids, solitary rocks and rugged ledges appeared everywhere in such profusion that it seemed impossible for a boat to be guided through in safety. The labour was great, but they accomplished it with great skill and success, until we had reached half way across the middle set of rapids, when a violent collision with a rock produced a leak which compelled them to pull up at a timber station that happened to be near and spend half an hour over repairs.

I remarked that in one part the bed of the rapid was composed of slate, which judging by the height to which it extended on the banks, had suffered a tremendous amount of denudation. The rocks which showed above the stream were of a harder slaty shale. Farther on, at another point in the rapids, the basement rock was undoubtedly trap. All that was seen was rough, pointed, and jagged. Nowhere had it yielded to the force of the running stream and become smooth. Dykes of it rose out of the water, bold and naked to the air, evidently denuded on both sides of the softer rock which formed its bed once, but had long since succumbed to the torrent. The small village we stopped at to make repairs was a very flourishing timber station. The hills at the back were well covered with fine fir trees, and a mountain stream flowed down from their inmost recesses, facilitating the transfer of the timber from these backwoods to the main stream.

October 2nd.—This morning I had the misfortune to be completely prostrated with a severe attack of dysentery accompanied by acute pain which lasted for some hours. I was obliged to stop the boat for four or five hours in order to ascertain the course which the malady was likely to take, harassed all the time with the thought of being compelled to relinquish my mission and return to Hankow crestfallen. However, to my great relief, the disease was quickly and completely driven away by opium and ipecac pills, the efficacy of which in the early stage of this malady I can thankfully vouch for. Having lost so much time, we only progressed 35 li for this day's journey. Although the disease was cured, I was left so utterly weak as to be unable to rise without assistance.

The events consequently of this day and the following week are written up from pencil notes jotted in my private diary, and from the journal kept by my writer.

October 3rd.—Started at 5 A.M., and reached Ch'ên-chou Fu, locally pronounced Shên-chou Fu, a distance of 70 li, by 7 P.M. I could not rise without assistance. From glimpses of the scenery I noted that high continuous hills on both banks hemmed in the river, and that they were well covered with tall straight fir trees and thick underwood.

October 5th.—Started early and passed a dilapidated city called Lou-ch'i Hsien, which had not yet recovered from the heavy hand of the " Longhaired Rebels " *i.e.* The Taipings. At 5 P.M. arrived at Pu-shih, formerly the flourishing centre of the timber trade, but now reduced to insignificance by its treatment under the rebel raid. The people, however, seemed to lack nothing in spirit, for they took all the trouble to make their way over fully a mile to where we were anchored off a stony flat, and upon our moving away they followed us along this most uncomfortable ground, shouting and using unpleasant expressions. Even the efforts of the Sub-Prefect who accompanied me in a gunboat were fruitless in quieting them, and as for the soldiers they positively feared the mob.

October 6th.—Started at daylight and reached Chên-ch'i Hsien, at 7 A.M. Just stopped long enough to exchange cards with the mandarin, and buy what provisions were procurable. The extreme difficulty of buying food has been a continual trouble to me the whole way. Fowl and duck are the only things to be had and in many places even these are not to be bought. More than this, such as can be bought are meagre and fleshless, containing no nourishment whatever. Any European, therefore, who attempts this route should provide himself with foreign provisions. At Chên-ch'i Hsien the river takes a most remarkable and provoking bend to the south of over 200 li, and then flows north, until reaching the line of its original course, it bends to the west again. This deviation forms a complete sack in appearance on the map, and adds greatly to the tediousness of tracking through innumerable small rapids.

* * * * * * * * * * * *

(This hiatus is unexplained.)

October 27th.—Reached Ch'ên-yuen Fu at 5 P.M. At the entrance of the city a good bridge of 5 or 6 arches, which would not disgrace a railway in England, spans the river. Rocky heights completely surround the town and lend a grandeur to its position. The gorge of the river for the last mile of our approach was very picturesque. On one side the rocks extended with such even regularity that they looked like the ancient walls of some Titan city, and the boatmen pointing upwards laughingly called them the city walls. On arrival, I immediately proceeded on foot, with my attendants and four men sent by the magistrate at my request to protect me a very short distance, to inspect an establishment in which I was intended to pass the night. It was not an inn, but a sort of forwarding house, of which several existed in the city, where travellers are not only lodged but provided with chairs, bearers, and ponies, for the overland journey. These rival establishments even take the trouble to send touts down the river in light swift boats to meet and secure probable customers. We were thus accosted the day before reaching Ch'ên-yuen Fu, but the person who presented the card disappeared as quickly as he came, instead of remaining with our boat. A circumstance which excited the comments of my attendants at the time, and somewhat puzzled me, though I thought nothing more of it. Although I had but a short distance to walk from the boat, a crowd quickly formed round me, principally consisting of soldiers, the fruitful source of trouble everywhere, and attempted to follow me into the house. But the very unsubstantial door was closed upon them, and it severely taxed the energies of the four Yamen men to keep it so. I examined the place and found a number of clean compartments made of new wood and divided off like horse boxes. Knowing the filthiness of Chinese inns, I thought the place a paradise, and immediately gave orders for the luggage to be brought in. But to my utter astonishment I was told that the mob in the rear would not permit a single box to be moved, at the same time excited shopmen rushed in by some back entrance, and protested that the mob in front had completely blocked in their shops and a stop to all business. Under these circumstances I resolved at once to go to the Hsien (Magistrate) and demand protection. Accordingly the door was opened, and the press fell back on seeing me advance. I walked through the mob unmolested and entered the Yamen, which was not a hundred yards away from the scene of disturbance, yet no effort had been made to repress the mob!! I was shewn into a small room, and had not to wait long before the Magistrate came in. His manner was rude, and a glance at his face told me that he was a type of the worst class of mandarins. He sat with face averted, and directly I began my complaint in quiet civil tones, burst out into a horse laugh and began to make excuses for the people. I immediately assumed an angry tone and told him it was no laughing matter, that he was Magistrate, and I expected him to disperse the mob, and find me a quiet lodging. I then showed him my passport and the Yamên's letter to the Governor-General. His manner instantly changed, and he gave orders to his men to go down, and guard the house in question. He then prepared a chair for me, in which I made an attempt to return. The crowd, however, was too great and aggressive for all the Magistrate's men, and we had to beat a retreat to the Yamen again, in which ignominious flight I had to be carried backwards through the mob. I was put under the necessity of breaking one man's nose who had the temerity to put his head inside the curtain of the chair to insult me. Attempts were made to upset the chair, but these were frustrated by my escort. As an example of Chinese official apathy, I may as well mention that at the very spot where I was being insulted by the mob, a military mandarin of high rank was passing by under whose very command were half the rioters around, and yet he made no more effort to repress them than a private individual. The result was that I had to sleep in the Magistrate's yamen. Under cover of night, bedding and food were brought up from the boat, and my cook soon provided me with a scratch dinner. " It is an ill wind, &c." But for the disturbance I should have had to waste two days in the city making preparations for departure, and striking ruinous bargains for men and conveyances. All this trouble was taken off my hands, for the Hsien was so anxious to get rid of me that he hired the men and ponies that very night so that, I might start early. In fact, he wanted me to go on ahead and leave them to forward my luggage. But I would not hear of such a plan, and arranged instead to move up beyond the city in the boat to a safe point where the carriers could meet us and the luggage be removed without hindrance.

October 28th.—Rose at daylight and went on board the boat before the city was astir. Moved up to the rendezous, and had everything safely transferred to the carriers, by 9 o'clock. It rained the whole day, and the high road, which was a narrow ill paved path, became dangerously slippery. In many places the highway to the capital was in a most disgraceful state of neglect. We met a great number of carriers and several strings of ponies returing from the capital, mostly empty-handed and unladen, whose presence, nevertheless, and the well worn path indicated a brisk trade along this route. Indeed, I was told by more than one mandarin that large quantities of opium, and the mineral products of Kwei Chou and Yun Nan were conveyed by this road into Hu Nan. But the expenses of carriage are very heavy, and neither road nor river, above Chang-tê Fu, can ever be of any use for foreign commerce. The whold country showed signs of having been recently devastated by the wild Miautze. All the villages had a new appearance. The cottages and shops were faced with clean fresh looking woodwork, and in the more prosperous houses, which were principally inns, carpenters were busily employed adding rooms and accommodation. The latter was of the rudest description, for I could see the sky at dawn, as I lay on my couch, through fifty gaps between the roof and the sides of the tenement; which added to the bitterness of turning out at daybreak with the thermometer at about 50°, and discomfort all around.

October 29th.—After proceeding about 12 li, we arrived at Shih-ping Hsien, where I went straight to the Magistrate's yamen, and was well rewarded for my visit. An exceedingly agreeable and gentlemanly man the Magistrate proved, and in the course of half an hour, we became great friends. He begged me to stay and spend the day with him, but I was obliged to excuse myself on the plea of extreme urgency to continue my journey. He regaled me with some delicious sweetmeats, made by his womenkind, and was good enough to present me with some on leaving, in return for which I gave him cigars. The city was, like the rest, reduced by devastation to a straggling hamlet. The Yamên itself was newly built, and stood alone as it were out in the country, on a site once surrounded by a busy population.

October 30th.—The road was fortunately dry to-day, for it wound through many dangerous places. The surefootedness and endurance of the chairbearers, who had frequently to carry my weight up long steep inclines and down precipitous paths, in which the stones were so irregular that I could not have walked down myself with their speed, often fairly astonished me, although I had been frequently carried over far worse places in Formosa in a similar manner. Two men bore the front shafts of the sedan, and one alone with a long leverage of poles sustained the weight behind. At a distance of 30 li I reached Hsin Chou and stopped at an inn to have my lunch, intending to call on the mandarin afterwards. But just as I had finished, a messenger arrived from the Yamên to say that a room was ready for me, and with a request that I would go up, which I immediately complied with. There being no resting place ahead which could be reached to-day, I readily accepted the hospitality of the very civil mandarin, with whom I had a most amicable conversation. He was a Canton man, and had both seen something of foreigners, and travelled by steamers. I omitted to mention an important incident which occurred yesterday. About midday two of my late boatmen appeared on the scene with a story that the mob at Ch'ên-yuen Fu, finding their bird flown on the morrow, wreaked their vengeance on the boat which had assisted in my escape. They had, according to their account, burnt all the covering and panelling of the boat, and besides this had destroyed three boxes belonging to me, which I had entrusted to the head boatman to take back to Hankow in order to lighten myself for the land journey, which was expensive in direct ratio to the weight of one's luggage. They also had a story to the effect that one of the rioters had let out that they intended to attack us down the river, but were prevented by the sight of the Taotai's gunboat. The man who gave us the hotel card and made off so suddenly, had an armed boat's crew in ambush to attack us at night. The head boatman came up with us in the evening, and gave a truer version of the story, by which I learned that my boxes were safe. I wrote a letter to the Magistrate at Ch'ên-yuen Fu, enclosing the boatman's deposition, and requesting him to examine into the matter, punish the offenders, and send me an answer at Kuei-yang. This outrage would not have occurred a few days earlier, before the late prefect left, on promotion to the rank of Taotai. His successor had only been in office two days, and was as yet unknown to the citizens of Ch'ên-yuen Fu. This turbulent place appears to have given trouble to many successive prefects, until the above mentioned officer, whose name is Wu, proved himself to be the only man able to rule the place, and this with so much popularity.

that the people would scarcely let him leave the city when he was promoted. I had heard of him at Chang-tê Fu, and obtained an introduction to him from a friend of his, but unfortunately I arrived just too late to benefit by his magnanimity.

October 31st.—The road passed at a very high level for nearly the whole of to-day's stage. The valley below seemed to be sparsely cultivated with rice, and large tracts of land remained in a wild state of nature. Slept at a place called Ta-fêng T'ung.

November 1st.—Shortly after leaving Ta-fêng T'ung, or the Cave of the Winds, we came upon the cave, which gives its name to the village. It had a very wide entrance, and I penetrated fully a hundred yards before it began to narrow. Water flowed down an artificial course from its inmost recesses to irrigate the fields outside. I had neither the time nor the means to penetrate further. The Chinese said it extended several li, and was full of water. In the course of two or three hours we reached Ch'ing-p'ing Hsien, which like the other was also a city of the dead, but had recovered itself in a much greater degree. Double the number of houses had risen up in comparison with the previous cities I passed through. I went to call on the Magistrate, but he was away. His servants, however, pressed me to go in and rest, an offer I readily accepted, as the chairbearers were about to have their breakfast, an operation which generally took up more than half an hour. They brought me tea, and three or four bowls of food, which I hungrily devoured with the help of chopsticks. On leaving the town I noticed a large heap of good coal exposed for sale, which clearly indicated the existence of mines in the neighbourhood. Every village I passed through showed sad signs of the savage havoc caused by the raid of the Miautze. Everywhere extensive remains of good substantial stone houses pointed out the prosperity that must have been, and in their stead twenty years of peace and quiet had only produced a huddled group of poor straw thatched huts inhabited by immigrants from Ssŭ Ch'uan and Kiang Si. Curiously enough there are signs of a sudden impulse of prosperity now taking place, for in every village, town, and city new houses were either just finished or in course of construction. Of trade there is nothing to speak of in any of these places, and every house is an inn with a small shop facing the street. I certainly benefited by the building mania, for I was sure of clean fresh quarters at night, although the mud floor could not, to use a simile employed by a mandarin who was eulogising Shanghai to me, be compared in cleanliness to the very streets of our model settlement.

November 2nd.—The road passed through a very fertile and beautiful, but wholly deserted, region. Large tracts of good arable land were given up to grass and wild weeds. This fact alone speaks very plainly of the wide-spread desolation, when we consider how accustomed the Chinese are to cultivate their very mountains up to almost inaccessible heights, and if the desolation is so great on the main road, what must it be in the less frequented interior. The Miautze have been taught many severe lessons by the imperial troops since their day of triumph, and indeed many of them now live in the cities I have passed through, mixed up with the Chinese population. I saw several of their women about the streets. A wild fearless look was in their faces, and withal a very attractive expression, such as I have seen in the countenance of the Pepohwan tribe in north Formosa. But whether throughly subdued or not, the settlers in the rising villages have little to fear from their lawless neighbours, for a chain of forts has been erected at distances of 5 li apart, each containing 5 soldiers, which serve as watch towers while the whole route is chock full of soldiery. This system is entirely owing to the energy, and vigorous administration of the late Prefect Wu, of whom I have spoken above.

November 3rd.—Just as the cities grow in size and start into more active life as we approach the capital, so the country becomes less neglected, villages appear in secluded hollows off the main road and every level plot is cultivated with rice. One crop had just been gathered in, and the patient peasant was everywhere engaged in ploughing up, with aid of the lumbering buffalo, the diminutive basins into which their paddy fields are divided, and preparing the ground for a second or third crop. I noticed a few men thrashing out the in-gathered grain with the very identical old flail which our farmers had to use before machinery drove it out of use. The only other object of cultivation which I could see anywhere was the tobacco plant. It was in blossom with a pink bell-like flower. I must not omit to remark that we met several hucksters on the road, carrying live stock, and among them were not a few baskets full of nice fat young puppies. On remarking to my head servant that they were evidently for market, and that I was not aware his countrymen ever indulged in dog flesh, he replied with considerable scorn " I should think not indeed; these young pups are for the Miautze who do eat them." At the end of 45 li or say 15 miles, we reached a city called Kwei-ting Hsien, which was, as usual, somewhat in advance of its neighbour in resuscitation. I went straight to the Yamên and was very civilly received by the mandarin, who had been at Shanghai and Tientsin, and could not refrain from praising up everything that was foreign. We were to go on to-day a long stage of 65 li, so in order to save time, I hurried away, thinking my baggage was well on its way. But what was my astonishment on descending to the main street to find the whole crowd of bearers in a regular mutiny. I had to get out and expostulate with them, surrounded all the time by 50 or 60 of the town's people who rather took my part and were exceedingly civil. I was surprised to find that here, as elsewhere, all along the route, the Peking dialect was thoroughly intelligible and that I could understand the people far better than I did in Hu Nan. The populace so far has proved itself quiet and harmless, always excepting Ch'ên-yuen Fu, which is a very pandemonium.

My expostulations resulted in the headman writing out a guarantee that they should carry me to the capital in exactly the same time under penalty of a heavy mulct. With this security I was content to remain, and having found comfortable quarters, revelled in my spare time to write up my correspondence.

November 4th.—In order to keep their promise, my troublesome carriers would have me rise unusually early, as they intended to "do" 75 li this day; of their accomplishing which I certainly felt very sceptical. However they did complete the long stage by 6 P.M., and I soon found myself in the yamên of the Magistrate of Lung-li Hsien.

This gentleman seemed to dread a meeting with the foreigner, and coolly sent a message of "Not at home," going into his back garden meanwhile with mistaken conscientiousness. However a note explaining my mission speedily brought him to his senses, and he not only sent a couple of men to escort me, but came himself in mufti, late at night, after I had finished my dinner, and smoked a few cigars with me, besides imbibing a little wine and some coffee, which he tasted for the first time in his life and seemed to enjoy. The road, for the greater part of the way to-day, passed through narrow ravines where the grass-clad hills approached very close and no room for cultivation intervened. Thick hedgerows lined the highway, composed of what in other countries are forest trees, but here meanly doing duty as stunted shrubs. There were the oak and the horse-chestnut of which I could not see even a moderately grown tree anywhere. Fine young Scotch firs were springing up everywhere, and crowning the hills with a fine deep green. Willows and ashes, sycamores and poplars (not the English kind) filled the lower slopes, and now and then I came across a magnificent Spanish chestnut. But the glory of the plain was the persimmon tree, all ablaze with the brightest yellow autumn tint. Wild flowers abounded everywhere, including the camelia, blue bells, marguerites, in splendid variety and profusion, and the violet. The whole road was a perfect paradise of ferns, and grasses flourished in marvellous variety.

November 5th.—To-day we have completed our last stage and entered the capital of Kwei Chou. I am delighted with the place. The people are most civil and not in the slightest degree troublesome. Although the streets were crowded none attempted to follow or stare. A look of astonishment passed over their faces, and that was all, while I more than once heard the civil expression used, "Oh here's a guest arrived." The main street, through which I had to pass on my way to the inn where my servant had secured lodgings for me, was exceedingly picturesque with its sign-boards, and dyed cloths exposed for sale, and coloured umbrellas spread out to tempt the rain with glittering red or blue or green. The first view of the city from the top of the last pass is very beautiful. It rests on an uneven plain well supplied with trees and completely surrounded by high hills, many of which stand solitary on the plain in remarkable forms. There were natural fortresses faced with smooth black rock at the top, otherwise clothed in rich vegetation, and which had been cleverly seized upon by bonzes to build imposing temples up in the air. Then again there was a perfect plum pudding and several pyramids with remarkably pointed apexes. The inequalities of the ground raised all the imposing buildings above the veil of the walls, which everywhere in China provokingly hide every vestige of a city from the traveller's approaching view. The last mile of the road was literally overloaded with memorial arches of white marble, or other subtitute, in perpetual honor of maidens distinguished for piety, and widows constant to the memory of the deceased. Their distant effect certainly added to the liveliness of the scene.

November 6th.—Having on hand a great many things to do to-day, I have been much hampered by a number of visitors coming in one after the other to ask the same questions, and examine everything I have with me that is strange to them. However much it may have benefited my knowledge and study of the Chinese, and of their intricate language, it certainly taxed my patience to keep up a conversation so long, and my palate to have to promiscuously drink tea and wine, and smoke cigarettes with perpetual relays of visitors. But at any rate I feel some satisfaction in having enlightened their gross ignorance, (although they were all of the literati class and expectant mandarins,) with regard to our position in China, the rank of our representative at Peking, and the good will which prevailed at the capital between the two nations. I called on the Governor of the Province at noon, by appointment, and was most civilly treated by him. A brisk old man, full of energy and intelligence, entered the reception hall after I had waited about a quarter of an hour for him. It was a large room and two sides of it were panelled with glass windows through which I should think there were fully fifty faces peering in during my interview with the great man. There were lesser mandarins in full fig, and a crowd of household servants. We sat midway up the hall on opposite sides more than twenty feet apart. A visitor of high or equal rank, he would have conducted to the divan at the upper end of the room. My first object was to borrow money, which was readily granted, and the next morning a parcel of silver ingots amounting to Tls. 130 or about £40 duly came to hand. I laid the case of the Ch'ên-yuen Fu outrage before him, begging for redress on behalf of the boatman, and requesting him to have issued a proclamation forbidding the people to molest English officials and travellers in future. He promised to give directions to Wu Taotai, the late Prefect of Ch'ên-yuen, to settle the matter, and plunged into an animated explanation of the probable cause of the disturbance. He said that Roman Missionaries were the only foreigners the people ever saw or came in contact with, and that as there had been a collision with them rather more than a year ago, when the mob destroyed a dispensary which the mission had established in the city, he thought it very probable that they mistook me for one of the same party returned to make another essay. On taking my leave, the great man, for such he is in very truth among his host of lesser officials, of whom there are several hundred in the capital, did me the honour of conducting me to my chair, which was twice as far as most mandarins of far lower rank would have condescended to move. I also called on the celebrated Taotai Wu, to press the Ch'ên-yuan Fu matter, thinking it very necessary for the sake of future travellers or pioneers of commerce coming that way that the mobbing propensity of the people should be thoroughly checked. The Taotai had a fine intellectual face and a benevolent eye. He said very little on the subject then, but on returning my call, some hours later, told me he had seen the Futai, and promised freely to carry out my wishes and to have the boatman indemnified. My time was completely occupied all the rest of the day in making arrangements to lighten my baggage and to travel more quickly. Being behind time several days, I was anxious to get on as fast as possible, but I found it quite impossible to cut short my stay at the capital under two days, and I was further interrupted by incessant visitors, whose continual "coming" did not cease till midnight. My expenses from Ch'ên-yuan Fu were far greater than they would have been had I been able to arrange through my servants. But under the circumstances, I was completely in the hands of the Magistrate, who hired carriers for me. I now determined to have nothing to do with carriers, but to put everything on horse-back so that no delay might occur from short fatigue stages. My servant called my attention to certain strong baskets which were used here to carry loose packages, and we found that by discarding boxes and separately packing their contents into these creels, the load of three ponies was reduced to two. By this lucky discovery I was able to effect a considerable saving. The hire of a pony carrying 160 lbs. was from 3 to 4 mace a day, or say 1s. 10d. to 2s. 6d. per day. That of a carrier, 2 mace or 1s. 3d. per day. Two men carried the load of one pony.

November 7th.—The whole day was taken up in packing and fixing the baskets and boxes to the pack-saddles, which on the morrow would be lifted on to the ponies when they were ready to start. I should have mentioned that at the instance of the Governor, the Magistrate or Chih-hsien had invited me to remove from the inn to an official dwelling, but the place was unfit to live in, and so I declined the honour. As he was in duty bound, this officer also sent me a fine haunch of mutton (goat) and a fowl. He returned my call and was most inquisitive. I had to take out everything I possessed of foreign make to satisfy his wondering gaze, but in spite of opera-glasses, breech-loading gun, revolvers, flasks and intricate despatch box, the palm was carried off by Sheffield cutlery, and the Magistrate amused himself like a child in cutting a sponge cake into pieces, which were speedily devoured by a half a dozen visitors in mufti. The table-knife had taken such a hold on his fancy, that this youthful official, (he was only about 30) disgraced himself by actually sending a messenger to ask for one of me, besides dropping many hints to my writer to the same effect. I refused his request on principle, veiled under the good plea of not being able to spare what I daily had in use. Much time was taken up in squaring accounts, for the exchanges in China are always intricate and varying at different places. Large cash were used in the country, but here in the city small cash of much less value were in vogue. I had also to do with lumps of silver, which required weighing and chopping into pieces. The Futai did me the honour to accept the present I sent him of cigarettes, liqueur, candles, and soap, sending in return a ham and some excellent tea called Pu-erh-ch'a, a celebrated product of Yun Nan. He had also the politeness to send me a letter of introduction to his son, who is a mandarin in Yun-nan Fu. Almost everything sold in the shops was brought from Ssŭ-ch'uan, particularly salt, silk, umbrellas and earthenware, but I could not ascertain what was exported in return. The invariable answer was that Kwei-chou produced nothing; and depopulated as it is I can well believe there is no special industry in the province.

November 8th.—Started rather late, owing to difficulties connected with the baggage; and consequently did not arrive at our first stage till after dark. Henceforth, we are to reach a city at the end of each stage, whether the distance be as short as 50 li, or as long as 90 li. We were now at Ching-chen Hsien, and the lateness of the hour deterred me from calling on the Magistrate. We exchanged cards, however, and he sent me a present of a fowl and a duck. Two official messengers were also detached to escort me to the next city, as the Futai had directed. The military commandant had the civility to send a couple of soldiers to escort me as well; an act of great respect, for, as my writer informed me, "the Emperor's troops might not be lightly moved." I should have mentioned that the same compliment was paid me at Kwei-yang, where two soldiers were sent to accompany me wherever I went.

November 9th.—Travelled 62 li to Ching-ch'i Hsien, and called on the Magistrate, who proved to be a somewhat jovial old man of 62. He had a very pleasant face, a very husky voice, and a chronic laugh tacked on to his words. I had the pleasure of receiving him later, after dinner, when he shewed a liking for sherry, and tried to smoke a long pipe of tobacco after trying both cigar and cigarette. The road was very wet and slippery after a shower, and it was by no means easy to have faith in the invariable sure-footedness of one's pony in the rough places and frequent inclines. In fact, mine did fall, without hurting his rider, however, which is fortunately the usual case with these small animals. The country was rather more colonised and cultivated than on the east side of the capital, but still vast tracts of level arable land, bearing distinct signs of former tillage, were completely deserted and covered with long grass. The villages on the main road are of a most miserable description, composed of huts built of the thick straw of the sorghum and plastered with mud or piled up with the stones and débris of former prosperity. They were far apart and contained a very few inhabitants, who were mostly immigrants from Ssŭ-ch'uan. In these villages, as on the previous route to the capital, food was spread on small tables at every door to attract passing coolies. But it was of a very inferior kind to that which was displayed to view on the eastern side of the capital. I could not find a decent room wherein to breakfast, and sat in the open air under the wondering gaze of the whole population. But everywhere the people were amenable and well behaved. It has been my habit to get out my writing materials whilst waiting for food, and the process always creates extreme astonishment. About midway on this day's route we crossed a very remarkable avenue of hills, extending in a straight line north and south for several miles, with a perfectly flat and narrow strip of fertile land between. Further on the general direction of the valleys was east and west. Wild flowers filled the road sides, and the tea-plant, in full blossom like a single camelia, grew wild all about the hedge rows, developed, untended, into a strong shrub eight or ten feet high.

November 10th.—On leaving Chin-ch'i Hsien, next morning rather earlier than usual on account of the longer stage of 80 li or 26 miles lying before us, the chief military officer, who was only of the rank of a *Ch'ien-tsung*, or say a lieutenant, not only had the civility to send a couple of soldiers to escort me, but gave me the usual salute of three detonating crackers as I passed the city gates; but more than this he paid me all the honours of a *Ta-jên*, or superior mandarin, by awaiting my arrival in full dress on the road, some two li beyond the gates. The ceremony took me by surprise, more especially as I was first made aware of his purpose by his card-bearer shouting out in loud tones, (as he dropped on one knee in the road and held up his master's official card,) that the *Ch'ien-tsung* had come out to pay his respects to his Excellency Mr. Ma. I dismounted and thanked the officer for his civility, but the brave soldier appeared to be so frightened by my condescension, that I remounted and passed on without more words. The whole route to-day passed through a fertile valley, perfectly level and some six to eight miles wide. It was only partially cultivated, for the country has not yet had time to recover from its 20 years of desolation. It was only last year that this main road become free from dangers and obstructions, and immigrants could come with safety to occupy the deserted wastes. The most remarkable feature of the Province is its hills. I have above noticed the singular detached cones and pyramids, which dot the plain of Kwei-yang Fu, (which by the way extends north and south,) but on leaving Ching-ch'i Hsien a regular conclave of these huge tumuli meets the view of the traveller. I cannot call them mighty, as the highest does not appear to exceed 300 feet. After passing through them we entered the fine valley above mentioned. It was bounded in its whole length along the 80 li we travelled to-day, by these same detached hills. They were not contiguous, nor in any way barred progress in between or round them in almost any direction; indeed long arms of the broad valley were seen to penetrate like estuaries through their midst. Far away in the southern boundary of the valley, where the hills seemed to be massed almost into a mountain range, the eye could still see similar separated peaks, which strengthened the presumption, that a very large belt of country was here both easily penetrable, and abounding in a complete network of small arable valleys. We reached the Prefectural city of An-hsün by six o'clock. The undulating downy ground to the east of the city, i. e. from the side we approached, was one vast grave-yard extending over two or three thousand acres. I never saw such a large collection of funeral mounds. Either this must have been a favourite cemetery, or the population of An-hsün Fu must have been enormous. The city is certainly very full of houses, and presents an animated appearance on entering the gate. It is built in a deep hollow, so that the gates overlook its entire area. I was too tired to visit the local officials, and we merely exchanged cards and civilities. The inhabitants were as well behaved as those of the capital. This city was strong enough to resist the inroad of the Miautze, who carried their ravages up to its very walls.

November 11th.—Left An-hsün at about 9 A.M., and passed through the same scenery surrounding the rich valley above-mentioned. Cultivation increased as we proceeded westward, and large tracts of fine rich soil were turned up to view by the plough. Villages were certainly more scarce, for we passed over 15 li without seeing any, but small groups of two or three huts, far away off the main road, sheltered the new colonists. As we approached the city of Chên-ning Chou, 60 li from An-hsün, the hills north and south began to approach nearer, and to close in upon the valley. For 140 li we had followed a level track, and indeed from Kwei-yang to this point, a distance of nearly 90 miles, the construction of a railway, should commerce one day require it, would be as simple and inexpensive as in any other part of the Empire. One thinks of Kwei Chou as an impenetrable mass of mountains, but it was most agreeable to find it possessed of many fine plains lying in the right direction. A nearer view of the conical hills brought to sight their rocky construction. Although vegetation climbed over their summits, yet the black craggy rock showed itself through the cloak. In most cases this weather-beaten sand-stone broke out in even concentric circles from base to summit, giving the hill a fortified appearance, or at a distance a rich fluted look. But in a few instances a complete eruption of knotty crumpled boulders covered the whole surface like a disease. We passed several Miautze women toiling along the road with very heavy loads for market, and shortly after came upon their picturesque retreats. These people perch their villages up on hills at a considerable height, and mostly choose out inviting spots where trees and shelter afford the best sites.

November 12th.—About 15 li from Chên-ning Chou, we came to the end of the fine valley, but entered another smaller one after crossing an easy pass. The hills now began to unite, but while their bases were welded together, the summits still preserved their individuality in conical peaks rising out of the mass below. In 10 li more the valleys came to an end, and the road wound in and out among low grass-covered hills; the rocky mountainous peaks having disappeared for the time being. We entered the village of Hwang-kwo-su, once a large town, over an old bridge of several arches, under which flowed a considerable body of water, after dashing down a series of small sloping falls. The village was half way, and I had my tiffin there. On leaving the place a grand sight met my view. There was the river, a couple of hundred yards below the bridge, leaping down a precipice of 140 feet in one of the prettiest falls I ever saw. The bank was wide, and the waters descended in two separate torrents, each of which would excite admiration by itself. The brown muddy look of the rock, over which the river flowed, added to the striking effect of the whole. From this point the road entered a mountainous pass, full of ups and downs. Far below was a deep ravine through which a stream flowed, but I could not see whether it was the same river I have just spoken of. Right out of the depths rose up a mighty wall of rock, topped as before by the comb-like row of peaks; while on our side a huge denuded rock, weather beaten and scored with streaks, leant over as if to peer into the canyon down below. It was a fine picture, and caused a refreshing thrill to pass over me as I looked on. Ten li further, and we gradually descended into another plain and entered the town of   where we took up our lodging at a new inn, which consisted of a wooden frame work, thatched roof, and bamboo laths neatly plaited together forming divisions to the rooms. The walls were not yet built nor plaster and ceiling added inside. Thick mats spread around and above served every purpose for temporary accommodation, and I must say I felt as warm as I wished with the thermometer at 55°. This is their way. They first build just the skeleton of a house, and then add on one necessary portion after another according as in course of time they earn enough money to afford it. This inn will no doubt become complete in the course of some months, but by that time it will have lost all the charm of cleanliness derived from its fresh bamboo laths, new woodwork and inviting mats, which combined to make me feel very comfortable. The climate of Kwei Chou is very temperate in November, else I should have been miserable enough in these new tenements half open to the sky.

November 13th.—The damp white mist, which has surrounded us for a day and a half, was to-day condensed into the still more uncomfortable form of fine rain, and the thick vapour floated low above the ground. It made travelling both difficult and dangerous, for the stone-paved or rather stone-strewn track, was provokingly rough in itself, but to-day, for fully ten miles, we passed a mountainous barrier over which the road ascended and descended somewhat steep inclines. But even in the midst of this mountain mass, where the rocky cones were tossed and tumbled like a stormy sea, there was a succession of quiet valleys down below lying flat at the base of these abrupt boundaries. To this region there succeeded a milder track of undulating, grass-covered wastes, enclosed by moderate hills fit for pasture, which led down into another broad valley, through which we travelled on level ground for 30 li, to the city of Lang-tai, which is denominated a T'ing, an order of jurisdiction ranking a little higher than a Hsien or Magisterial Government. There are but few of them in the Empire, compared with the regular departments of Fu, Chou, and Hsien. If a direct road were possible to Yun-nan Fu, four or five days might be saved in the transit, but our route to-day proved how tortuous it will continue to be for the next five days, until we reach the plains of Yun Nan. The road is almost deserted by commerce. For miles we have met no goods passing or repassing. Of travellers there are a few. Evidently little trade has risen as yet by this route between the two provinces. There *is* some, however, for on the *whole* way from the capital, I have noticed three or four consignments *en route ;* native cloth and straw hats going west, and lead and tea to the capital, were distinguishable amongst them at a glance.

November 14th.—We left Lang-tai this morning with the promise of a short stage before us, which was a gratifying prospect, as it was raining still and a leaden sky gave no hope of change. The road was extremely slippery, and in many parts almost dangerous either for riding, chairing, or walking. A fresh escort of two soldiers came in exchange for those from the last stage; I was thus forwarded on from place to place : but in every case I had to deliver the last passport and to make a request for the men. Everywhere, however, I have met with the greatest civility, deference, and even something approaching to obsequiousness. Lang-tai was full of houses and struggling hard to recover from its long depression. At this place I first began to discover that there was a Kwei Chou dialect, which sufficiently diverged from the Peking tongue to puzzle both me and those I addressed to entirely understand each other. From this I inferred that there must be a smaller admixture of Ssu-ch'uan men in these parts; an inference I might almost have drawn from an absence of the brisk geniality and readiness which marks the people of the latter province. For the Kwei Chou provincial is a dull heavy featured being, and hopelessly addicted to smoking Yun Nan opium. Although our stage was short, it proved to be doubly tedious, as we entered a really mountainous region at last, and the road was full of steep inclines. After crossing a low ridge we skirted a fine valley for about two miles, at a great height above it, looking over a rich scene of cultivation and agricultural revival. After this we suddenly got locked in among the hills and rose higher and higher until we stopped to breathe at the very summit of a short rocky range, running N.W. and S.E., which fairly barred the way. My aneroid marked 3,400 feet above the sea, or rather Shanghai, (which is much the same thing), but I cannot trust its accuracy. A glorious sight was seen on the other side. We were on a level with the majority of peaks massed together right and left, and far below lay a small plain to which we had to descend by a very steep path. Masses of white mist floated below and for a time obscured the fine panorama. But we were up in clearer air, and it no longer rained. The descent was difficult and slow. At the half-way-down house, where the steepest parts came to an end, I again looked at my barometer and found we were 1,400 feet below the splendid point of view we had just left, which seemed incredible. While scanning the mountains from above I estimated that the average height of the highest ranges was about 4,000 feet. From the half-way village (of two huts), where we had to breakfast, the road wound down over a length of some 2 miles till we reached another plain little cultivated, but strangely enough, full of large villages; and shortly reached our halting place, which did not boast of a proper inn. I have to sleep in a mat shed with a pigsty alongside. But the barn-like structure is roomy and airy, and the temperature is high, or I should perish with cold. Being well guarded against pet Chinese "luxuries," by insect powder, clean mat, india-rubber sheet and air bed, I can lie down as calmly as a sybarite at home. The aneroid has fallen further to 1,500 feet. To-morrow, we are led to expect the hardest day's march of the road, and I anticipate a second ascent to the skies. I must not omit to state that within the first 15 li from Lang-t'ai, we crossed a coal bed which cropped out abundantly on the surface. There were large blocks of solid coal bared to view, and the bank of the highway was a mass of coal dust, which the settlers simply scraped into their baskets and carried down to town for sale. We met several women bent on this errand with light loads, before reaching the source of their wealth. It may be worth mentioning that the rocky ranges which were grouped about the high ridge we crossed, one and all presented a grass-clad mild appearance towards the north and east, but on looking back at the towering summits from the valley, I noticed that vegetation stopped short within about a hundred feet of the top, facing south and west, and that a precipice of bare, black rock gave a sharply defined outline to the crest. White streaks also marked this rugged face, as though it had been irregularly whitewashed.

November 15th.—Mê-k'ou, our resting place last night, was only a village, and to-day's stage of 35 li has brought us to another village named H'ua-king. These places have not yet recovered their former size and importance on the main road. A river flows past Mê-k'ou beside a dark pebble strand where the people of the place pick up bits of sand-stone prettily streaked with quartz, (for the latter has reappeared in this region), which they cut and polish to sell to travellers. I gave

50 cash, or about 2d, for a piece which would have cost a shilling at Brighton, and incurred the moral censure of one of my chairbearers, who could not get over such a show of extravagance for a long way, as I gathered from his remarks to the other men. This will serve to shew how poor the Chinese are, and how far a few copper cash will go with them. A respectable gentleman only pays 100 cash for board and lodging per night at an inn; that is, about 4d. I bought half a sheep at Ching-ch'i Hsien for a tael and a half, or nine shillings, which was at the rate of 3½d. per pound. It is sufficient to cumshaw an official messenger who has walked twenty miles in the rain for you with the handsome sum of four-pence, which will make him K'o-t'ou with joy; a Chinaman would give him two pence. Coolies and bearers can eat and drink their fill for 3d. Many a gentleman is well off with Tls. 25 a year. Imagine an income of £ 8.6.0 sufficing. My literatus will wrangle for two cash with the poor roadside purveyors. He will also go for any given time without a bath, sleep in the same room with filthy coolies, smoke their dirty pipes, and do an infinity of other unnecessary acts of condescension, which mark China as the true home of Democracy, and the place where Fraternity and Equality have taken root with advantage to the lower orders, but at the expense of a good deal to the more respectable classes. Yet, in ceremonious etiquette, this dirty pauper will claim equality with any one, and seem the polished gentleman.

As I anticipated, our road was full of rises to-day, and the aneroid marks 3250 ft. The temperature has consequently fallen several degrees, and I am lodged in a worse barn than the last miserable place. Not to speak of dirt and odours and the damp muddy floor, I have the cooking place on my left hand, sending its smoke from the centre of the floor throughout the barn, and the pack-horses stabled on my right, a little further removed by the blessing of an intervening compartment in which my servants sleep. We are boxed off by low partitions under a common roof. To return to the road. How the chairbearers managed to pass over the most impossible quagmires strewed with jagged stones, (displaced from the original pavement) and at an incline of over 40°, without even jerking me, was a marvel. I could only sit rigid and await a collapse which it seemed impossible to avoid. The Viceroy of Yun Nan and Kwei Chou is on his way back from Peking, and will have to pass over this wretched track. It is to be hoped, as I overheard a bearer remark, that his experience or sufferings will lead to a mending of matters. I underrated the size of yesterday's valley. On rounding a hill I saw that it extended a long way and could afford ample occupation to the villagers. The whole plain was yellow with the rice stalks, and patterned out with good effect by the numerous meandering boundaries which banked up the paddy plots. A few acres were planted with the sugar-cane which had reached six or eight feet in height, and small attempts were made to cultivate cotton, which I likewise noticed in other places along our route to-day, but it was poor and growing short. Two high ranges running E. and W. bounded our horizon, while the intermediate space was valley to the south, and a grass-covered uneven plateau to the north fit for pasturage. Cattle are scarce, but carefully bred. The local authorities forbid their slaughter yet. There were trees over the hills. Deep red, yellow, and orange tints of autumn showed up with beautiful effect amid the mass of green. The sun had appeared at last and dispelled the mists. So that altogether the scene was very refreshing and the journey far less tedious.

November 16th.—The road to-day passed over a long stretch of wearisome hills covered with tall grass, without trees, without valleys, with only their endless rise and fall always hiding a view of the bold majestic peaks beyond. The river at Mê-k'ou I should have stated is the boundary of the wild-tribe settlements. They do not perch upon the hills this side of the stream, although their ravages were carried far beyond. Happily not a single bridge was destroyed in their sweeping rage, which spared neither monuments nor temples. Many fine stone structures span the frequent ravines and rivers which must obstruct a mountain road. By enquiries made through my writer, who required some work, I learned something of these Miao-tzŭ, and other wild tribes in the hills, together with the causes of their insurrection. There are two sets of social outcasts, the Miao-tzŭ, and the Chung-chia. The former, although they assimilate both in dress and general features to the Chinese, just as the Shans beyond Yun Nan, described by Dr. Anderson, never belonged to the celestial race. They were the aborigines of this region at the time when the Han dynasty (B.C. 202 to A.D. 200) extended the Empire westward, and colonised this province from Hu Nan. The Chung-chia are the descendants of those colonists. Both "nations" have several subdivisions distinguished by little peculiarities of dress, and are mostly called by names describing the same. I saw representatives of three or four sects, and could easily see the difference. For instance, there are the White Miao; the embroidered Red Miao; the Black Miao, (who by the way wear earrings as well as black clothes; The men but one, the women both); the Light-Blue Miao; the Flowered Miao, (who wear sleeves only of coloured stuffs like chintzes or brocades); and oddest of all, the Duck's-beak Miao (who wear a thing like a duck's beak on the back). The women are the badge bearers, the men doing as they like in the matter. But the latter mostly dress like Chinamen in the universal blue. The Chung-chia have three classes. The Pu-la-tzŭ, among whom the women wear pigtails as well as the men; the Pu-i-tzŭ, whose women wear silver plates on the head for caps,—*absit omen*,—I hope the thirst for novelty elsewhere may not adopt the hint; and the Pu-lung-tzŭ, distinguished by the coiffure resembling a raven. They all wear the Chinese garments but add a border of some other colour. These people exist in great numbers between An-hsün Fu and Mê-k'ou along the route we have followed. The Miao-tzŭ inhabit more generally the region between Ch'ên-yuan Fu and the capital. Judging by the state of the cities and the universal ruin, on that side and on this, I should say that the aborigines excelled the colonists in the fierceness of their onslaught. It was a combined movement, and the opportunity arose when the Mahommedans held Yun Nan, and the T'ai-p'ing rebellion overflowed Kiang Si and Hu Nan. The reason of this rising was not an idle one. The Chinese had oppressed both classes, socially as well as officially, and while the one said, "we are Chinese as well as you, and yet all honours, riches, and advantages are debarred us," the poor wretched Miao-tzŭ had to complain of scorn, contempt, and legal robbery in rents and taxes.

November 17th.—The night was cold in our barn, or rather shed. On rising I found the temperature to be 48° ; in the afternoon however, it rose to 60°. I was told by villagers that they have snow in winter. Their houses, built so open to the air, would lead one to an opposite conviction. But then these people never change their clothes night and day, and make up for the rest with cotton-quilts. The beds in the best inns are merely loose planks placed on log-wood tripods, and covered with dirty straw. Apparently the accumulated dust has never been disturbed, except where I happened to lie. Coal dust is in general use at the villages we pass through now, and to-day we crossed another bed of it, less distinctly marked on the surface. By compensation for yesterday's tameness, we were refreshed to-day along the whole route by the sight of smiling valleys full of life, and colour and cultivation. They did not lie so flat as those seen above, but seemed to grasp the undulating hills of red sandy soil, and cultivation was carried up in the familiar terraces to every available spot. Trees were plentifully scattered about and added to the beauty of the scene. There were the sycamore, the plane tree, the poplar and the Spanish chestnut; a pretty smooth-leaved holly covered with red berries, and the universal pine. The further we go west the more we find of cultivation and population. The villages increase on the road and there is more small traffic ; oranges from Yun Nan and straw shoes come along ; while drovers are met with flocks of sheep ; flying eastward, some say, from the cold weather in Yun Nan ; others to feed their flocks on the grassy hills of which I have spoken, pasture being scarce in Yun Nan. I cannot tell yet which is the true explanation. Baron Richthofen, in his able Report to the Shanghai Chamber of Commerce, states that from the information he was able to obtain, Yun Nan must be bitterly cold in winter. But I was repeatedly assured by natives of the Province, who came to visit me at the capital, that the temperature was mild and warm. Kwei Chou must have a temperate climate, for the houses are not built to guard against cold, and among other signs I notice that the horse-chestnut has not yet dropped its faded blossoms. So far the average temperature we have experienced has been about 55°. The droves of sheep have been recently shorn, and numbers of young lambs accompany the flock. The very young and tender ones are carried in felt blankets on the backs of the drovers.

I came in time to witness a curious domestic scene in a village. A small child was being flogged by his father. Both parents were engaged in the operation; the one to ply the besom and the other to meekly protect the little victim who dodged round her from one side to the other catching a stroke at each move. The mother stood with her back to the executioner and bore off the child as soon as she dared, pushing it forward gently with both hands; for the Chinese never drag young children along by the arm. The group was decidedly interesting, more especially as the scene was enacted in the street. Some people do these things in private.

November 18th.—We stopped last night at the town of Yang-shun, in clean but rather cramped lodgings. The traveller has to look out sharp for mandarins and others in company, for if they should arrive first and occupy the only good inn, his plight is rather hopeless. This was somewhat our case at Yang-shun, for a mandarin in charge of the repairs to the official resting house had already established himself in the best inn. The inhabitants appeared to be extremely poor, for I saw scarcely an individual whose clothes were not patched with native "buff" and their hovels are fearfully filthy. But they have a habit of spending their money on opium and even costly ornaments, such as jade for mouth-pieces to pipes. The barber of the town had given Tls. 2 for a piece of green jade for this purpose, a monstrous extravagance, in his condition. But he was decidedly better off than the rest, probably owing to the fact that shaving the head is a recurrent necessity to all. A similar example of childish extravagance occurred in the early part of my journey. One of my boatmen had spent Tls. 3 on a singing bird which appeared to be the sole object of his affections. After hours of tracking, perhaps in the rain, he would rush to the cage as eagerly as the rest to their meals. Yet the price was more than he could earn in a mouth in his hard calling.

The road passed through a number of valleys full of rice, and watered by small streams running in a North Easterly direction. The distance to the *Chou* city of Pu-an was only 40 li, which had to be accomplished in one stretch, as it was impossible to find a place fit to prepare breakfast in at the villages on the road. This was owing to the fact of our having quitted the main road in order to give the bearers and animals a day's rest in the city. This, however, was not granted after all, as I discovered that the men had deceived me in losing a day by making one short march. Another reason, which would have sufficed, was the absence of any accommodation in the city, and being lodged in the Ya-mên I was anxious to put the inmates to as little inconvenience as possible. The mandarin was away, and at first there was no admittance, a strong disposition being shewn by the servants to treat me with contempt. I was closely surrounded by a large crowd, which behaved well, but pressed uncomfortably. I was talking to an old man through the window of my chair, and on remonstrating against the rudeness of the people, he remarked that they had never seen such a thing as a glove before, and must he excused. I found my gloves everywhere the object of intense excitement. Under these circumstances there was no alternative but to enter the precincts of the Yamên in my chair and request to see the *Shih-yeh*, a gentleman who fills the post of *fidus Achates* to the Magistrate in every city, and is often tutor to his sons. In the present instance the *Shih-yeh*, proved to be a very sensible man. So soon as he had recovered from the trepidation caused by my bold intrusion, he was good enough to find quarters for me and all my incumbrances in the Yamên. The main road would have taken us to a place called ————————seven li to the northward of P'u-an Chou.

November 19th.—On leaving early this morning we met hundreds of men and ponies carrying coal into the city. It was mostly in dust, but a small quantity was in lumps of a useful size. Further on we saw the mine or narrow shaft from whence it was all procured. The shaft was driven at a downward incline, contrary to the usual practice in China. I don't know how they get rid of the water. About a mile from P'u-an, we began to ascend the last great barrier on our road. It was called the Yun Nan pass, and exceeded all the others in length. But the incline was easy, and the summit moderately high (3,300 ft.) There was no steep descent on the other side, the road passing over a high plateau of very poor land. Before reaching the crest of the pass I looked back on a lovely scene. The fine valley was decked out with autumn tints and harvest gold. The high hills all round were strown with large patches of red soil in among the trees, and the city with its crowded roofs and triumphal arches lay in a cradle below. The last half of the stage was barren ground; rocky rough low hills on both sides, and coarse grass growing among boulders in the middle. Towards the end however, we came across a beautiful valley in which all the harvest operations were over, and instead of yellow the sombre colour of rich earth relieved the eye. It had a comfortable look, as though the land had put on its winter clothing. The stage had been a long one, and the bearers, thoroughly tired out, dropped the chair with a well-feigned slip, and so compelled me to walk a long way in the closing darkness over an atrocious path. When at length I reached the inn it was full of smoke, and could not be cleared until the cooking was over.

November 20th.—We were now fifteen li from the boundary line of Yun Nan and Kwei Chou. The excitement of crossing the border and entering the famous Province, which filled us at starting, was rather damped by the morning rain, but by noon the sun shone out almost uncomfortably and dispelled the mists. The road sloped down easily over a red sand waste towards the frontier town, which was distinguished by an arch at each end of its single street. The first thing that attracted my attention was a cart. Here was the very baggage cart of Peking employed in agriculture and drawn by oxen or buffaloes. The view towards Yün Nan was disappointing. There did not seem to be any termination of the undulating rock-covered hills, which extended as far as the eye could see. But the road was level, and the hardened red sand made it firm and easy to travel on. Large pits and gullies exposed the red sand to a depth of fully forty feet. We met quantities of salt on its way to Kwei Chou, in symmetrical blocks of a spherico-triangular shape, and covered with mandarin "chops.*" There were also a good many men employed in carrying gypsum to the same destination. It is used in the preparation of bean curd, a favourite article of food. A short stage brought us to the first city of Yün Nan lying in our way; the magisterial city of P'ing-i Hsien, where I was received with marked incivility by the Mandarin (a Kiang Su man named Hsia.) It was a kind of rudeness which a Chinaman can so easily show without going far out of the way, and consists in using expressions applicable to an inferior, and omitting forms of etiquette which are held indispensable. He seemed to be suspicious of the local passport and examined the seal critically. I was able to cut all this short by reference to the Tsung-li Yamên despatches, and the letter of the Kwei-yang Fu-t'ai, which he owned to having received. He carried out his instructions, however, and sent two men as escort.

November 21st.—Our road to-day was beautifully level over the broad battened red sand. Still, barren wastes continued on all sides, well peppered with rocks and stones. One or two dry gullies abounded in quartz. The rocks were all rotten and disintegrated, just as they appeared in many places on the way, and more especially round about P'u-an Chou. At eight li from P'ing-i Hsien there is a remarkable cave on the left of the road. Its mouth had been filled up with a temple, which the Mahomedans destroyed, but the huge space of the cavern is still full of hideous figures of demons and deities perched up on ledges or bound to the bristling roof. There were small stalactites hanging from the vault. The decrepid priest said the cave had been penetrated to the distance of 3 or 4 li, but no gigantic bones or such-like deposits had been found. The upper part of the cavern was grey sandstone, below this I tested limestone, and red sandstone lay at the base. Before reaching our resting place, a town called Pai-shui, there intervened one fine plain at last through which a narrow stream flowed in a general northerly direction. The harvest was just over, and beans were shooting up between the stubble. In every village a lively scene met our view. One and all were engaged in either stacking the straw or wield-

*[Written characters indicating the places between which the salt was travelling, or the barriers it had passed.]

ing the flail. In Hu Nan and Kwei Chou they have a curious habit of hanging the straw on trees instead of stacking it on the ground. They select a tall young fir or any tree which is free of leaves for 15 or 20 feet, and suspend the bunch from a point in its trunk. The tree looks as if it wore a crinoline drawn up rather high. The plain was full of flocks of storks.

November 22nd.—The road to-day for half the stage passed over another plateau of waste uncultivable land on which there was little grass even, but a great quantity of rocks and stones. We noticed lumps of iron lying about of an almost pure quality. My writer ferretted out a story about some one having discovered lead incorporated with it; and that a number of his associates found it sufficiently remunerative for a short time to extract it on the spot in a rough way, but that they soon had reason to abandon so incomplete and rude a project. The soil everywhere on this plateau was very rich in variety. Underneath the all-pervading red there were calcareous deposits. Numbers of large boulders of pure chalk (?) lay about. There were several banks of clay of various colours, especially green and purple. The whole field was painted. But the region was nothing but a rough desert of undulating ground surrounded with hills. The latter half of the stage, however, beyond the half-way village of Hai-tzǔ P'u, improved in scenery and verdure. Wherever the rice harvest was being gathered in, the road was full of buffalo carts conveying the grain to the village. The people are not particular about choosing a clean threshing floor, and as often as not scatter the very street with grain and straw; and the street of a Chinese village is better left undescribed. But certainly the mud and dirt were dry, and the buffalos shied at my chair, and the pack-horses shied at the carts, causing a stampede, which excruciated my feelings over the possible fate of my filter and my wine. Each day I received the report of my servant with an inward groan. Glass and crockery went their way long ago, and yesterday, two precious bottles of brandy closed the list. On nearing the end of our journey, the plateau suddenly came to an end, and a very fine plain burst on our view. It stretched away to the south and widened as it went. The city of Chan-i Chou lay opposite us on the other side of the valley, about two miles off. The bearers, with the goal in view, redoubled their speed and almost ran me into the city. I sent my card to the mandarin; but here again the same sort of incivility was offered. No card was returned, and no answer could be obtained to a civil request that the escort might be sent early, since we had to start at daylight. As the mandarin probably knew little or nothing about all this, I sent my writer with the Treaty to enlighten this all powerful janitor and factotum on my position. The result was that he rated them soundly, (for the writer has been very prone to clothe himself with a little official pride on account of being attached to a small mission), and his lecture had the desired effect, for the Magistrate's card arrived by-and-bye with an answer to my request.

November 23rd.—After waiting in vain for an escort I started
without it, and had proceeded a long way before anyone came from the
Yamên. At length a stupid old man turned up, who proved very useless.
He was dressed in the garb of a common coolie, and I strongly suspect
had been hired out of the street for the purpose. His warrant only contained one name. So that instead of sending two or more men, as all
previous officials had readily done, they had taken the liberty at the
Yamên to change the number stated in the warrant, and so reduced me to
the certainty of having only one man sent for the rest of the route; for
they copy one another faithfully. But we are near the capital, the road
is good and the people are civil, so I do not pay much attention to this
want of courtesy. On starting from Chan-i we at first followed its
splendid valley due south for a mile or two, and then abruptly broke out
of it at right angles, to ascend a series of small, but uncomfortable passes
which led up to another dreary plateau, like those we have already passed.
The valley was well cultivated with rice, and the harvest being over, the
numerous flooded fields gave the appearance of a vast lake to the plain
as seen from above. Numerous flocks of storks found a good feeding
ground thereon. But a good deal of this space was really a swamp, and
not yet put to use. There were high causeways running in all directions, but many had fallen to pieces in different places. Their existence
seemed to indicate the occurrence of floods. We reached the city of
Ma-lung Chou in good time, and found a very fair lodging at the kung-
kuan. I sent a civil note to the mandarin announcing my arrival and
errand, and regretting my inability to call, on account of having injured
my foot. To this a verbal answer was sent, and as to the matter of an
escort, the example set by the previous Magistrate was of course followed,
except that a youth was sent to take care of me; but he was a decided
improvement on the old man.

November 24th.—Left Ma-lung Chou before sunrise in order to
complete 80 li in good time. The country improved in appearance by
the addition of trees, which, though stunted, grew abundantly on the hills
and plain, relieving the desertlike monotony of the red soil which still
continued. At the halfway village of Pai-tzŭ Pu, a Roman priest came
up to me suddenly as I was seated at one of the public tables, having
tiffin, and commencing in Chinese, continued in French that he was also
travelling to the capital, and was delighted to meet a foreigner. We
sat down together. But my reverend friend had so poor a larder that I
was obliged to supplement his bit of cold fowl with half my beefsteak,
and he was so delighted to see bread, that before he had finished his
repast I had no more to offer him. However, I made the cook serve up
an omelet for him, and a cup of cocoa, which was welcomed. As is very
common among missionaries, there was a rumour in his community of
hostile feelings having been exhibited against foreigners in the north
lately, and the rumour was tinged with a halo of imaginary massacre.

The cry of wolf is so often raised that foreign residents will speedily become indifferent to the reality some day. I also learned from this gentleman that there had been a disturbance at Yung-ch'ang Fu, which if true would cause me serious difficulty in passing through, but further inquiry proved that something much less imposing had occurred somewhere else, and that the matter had been long since settled.

November 25th.—We slept last night at the town of I-lung Ssŭ, and having another long stage of 75 li before us, left at daylight. Our fresh escort again consisted of a dirty-looking lad, who could be of no use whatever. The country was full of trees and underwood. Our road, always wide and level, passed through many lanes and hedge-rows. The wind, as usual every day, blew uncomfortably from the south-west, parching the skin of our faces and producing disorders of the throat. I noticed that it sprang up about 9 A.M., the earlier hours being still and undisturbed. Houses everywhere wore a neat and comfortable look. They were detached and roomy, built of sun-dried mud bricks and well tiled. But we no longer saw the open exposure to the air which distinguished those of Kwei Chou. Wind and cold were carefully shut out. On nearing *Yang-lin,* which was a town now, but must have been a city once, the road skirted a large lake covered in many parts by tall reeds. It was an immense expanse of water, and is said to afford quantities of fish. Soon after this a magnificent plain burst on our view, well studded with new villages, but swarming with ruins of old ones. We struck across the valley at right angles and entered the town of Yang-lin, where there were inns enough to accommodate several parties arriving in company with us.

November 26th.—On leaving Yang-lin the ruins caused by the war were sadly prominent. The area covered by houses was evidently very large, and from its splendid site, and quick revival, I should think this must have been an important city. The distance to the capital was 105 li, on a very level road ; so that it might be accomplished in one day, but as I wished to be well lodged in order to be able to complete my arrangements easily, I preferred to stop short of the capital, and sent my messenger on ahead to secure a good house. He was also charged with letters to the bank and the Yamên, reporting my arrival. We stopped at the town of Pan-ch'iao. It has several inns, but they are exceedingly bad. My room was choked up with smoke, but the excessive annoyance of this nuisance was no novelty by this time, for my eyes and throat have suffered not a little from its almost nightly repetition. Along the whole route I have had to struggle against wrong information. Distances and routes vary, apparently according to the ideas of different persons, and the result is that I have been misled to the extent of losing 10 days. Instead of 25 days being sufficient to accomplish the journey from Ch'ên-yuan Fu to Yun-nan Fu, I have only managed to reach the threshold of the latter city in 30 days ; and this after every effort to hurry my conductors. One more vexatious " fact " was accidentally learnt to-day in conversation, at the tiffin stage, with a very polite military mandarin who was travelling in the opposite direction. He had been to Yung-ch'ang Fu, and showed me stage by stage on the map that it took 20 stages to reach that city. Now I had been assured at Kuei-yang Fu, by men of the official class who had also been over the road, that there were only 11 stages. This discrepancy fills me with much anxiety as to the possibility of arriving at the rendezvous in good time.

November 27th.—Started early and reached the city before noon. My servant met me at the gates and conducted me to a very good official inn. The road was crowded with people passing to and fro. Carts conveying firewood, mingled with ponies carrying charcoal, jostled coolies coming out with loads of salt slung at the ends of their useful bamboo. The short suburb was full of saddlery shops, and the stalls displayed nicknacks, opium lamps, and ornaments. One solitary clock was the only representative of foreign ware which met my gaze. The people were not curious or troublesome, and I entered the city unescorted, without the slightest difficulty. There was nothing showy in the approach. Ruins surrounded the walls and dotted the magnificent plain stretching far away. The city is on level ground, and therefore not picturesque. A few very neat and original examples of roofing near the gates showed the best points of Chinese architecture.

November 28th.—Yesterday I had just had time to establish my self at the inn and unpack all my baggage in order to rearrange it, when a couple of messengers came from the Chih-hsien, inviting me to remove into the official quarters, which had been prepared, and by way of stopping all objection on my part, they urged that the Acting Viceroy had directed these arrangements, and that the Magistrate had sent a couple of men to meet me in the suburbs, but that they had missed me altogether. We moved accordingly into the temple where quarters were assigned to us, and found everything very clean and convenient; comfort however was marred by the absence of a paper covering to the windows and door. Thirty feet of open woodwork letting in the night air at a temperature below 50°, made us feel extremely chilly; and the only means of warming the room was a small brazier of glowing charcoal. This deficiency however was corrected by the paper-hangers, in the morning. A splendid double repast of choicest Chinese dishes was also sent down by the Magistrate, for me and my servants. Eight large wooden trays containing fifty six bowls of different dishes and sweetmeats, all ready for the cook's hands, met my view on entering the room, and four cooks from the Yamên were ready to operate. But as I had already dined, I requested them to come on the morrow and prepare the banquet at eleven. Accordingly this morning I invited my writer to help me to do justice to the rich viands, and we set to work with chopsticks and a keen relish. I never enjoyed a better dinner. A crowd of harpies in the kitchen fell upon the abundant remainder, and soon reduced it to nothing. After this I proceeded in my chair to call on the Magistrate, who received me very well, and pleased me so thoroughly in his appearance, bearing, and straight-forward manner, that I no longer cared to see the Governor, and entrusted all I wanted to him. He said if I particularly wished it, the Governor would appoint a place to meet me, but that he was very busy, and the Revenue Commissioner was engaged in handing over his charge to a successor; so that if I had no objection he, the Hsien, would attend to my wants, and convey messages to and from these high officials. I readily assented, and delivered the Yamên letter into his hands. My first object was to communicate with Col. Browne in case his party should arrive first, and to request the Acting Viceroy to send instructions post haste to the Yung-ch'ang Fu officials, to give him every assistance. And secondly, I asked for an escort for myself and a letter to all the mandarins *en route* explaining my position and object. The Magistrate, whose name is Pien, readily promised to convey my requests to the Viceroy, and so with warm thanks for his civility I concluded a very agreeable visit. I then went to the bank and drew out as much as I immediately required. Chinese money matters are hedged about with complications; not only do the intrinsic and artificial values of the sycee silver vary at every new place you arrive at, but the weights in vogue are as different as possible.

November 29th.—The Magistrate returned my call this morning and said that the Governor was extremely busy just now, but would be ready to see me when I came back from Yung-ch'ang Fu. He had deputed a couple of mandarins to escort me the whole way, and was about to send a flying despatch to Yung-ch'ang Fu, which would arrive in four days at that city, and my letter to Col. Browne would be forwarded by the same opportunity. The Magistrate further undertook to supply me with the necessary horses and carriers for my journey, and I had more than once to decline putting him to any such charges. After a long amicable visit, he left, begging me to rest assured that all would be well. In the course of the afternoon I received a message from the Governor requesting me to wait another day to allow time for the escort to get ready. I was obliged to acquiesce, although time was very precious. It is impossible to get things done promptly in China. I have not been able to go about yet, but by report I find everything is exceedingly dear in this city. Considering how lately it has been re-occupied, and the expense which has been incurred by every shop-keeper in opening his business, it cannot be wondered at that prices range high. Food also is dear, and porterage adds greatly to expenses. The fine plain which stretches away into the far distance, lies fallow for want of hands to cultivate it, and numberless ruins of villages mark the devastation of the late war.

November 30th.—I was led to expect a visit from the escorting mandarins to-day, in order that we might become acquainted, but as no one came, and nothing further was heard of arrangements for starting to-morrow, I called on the Magistrate late in the day to take my congé and impress it upon him that I was to start next morning. The fact seemed to wake him up as if he had not realized it, for he had neglected to inform the deputed officials of my haste. His mind was full of the coming magnate, and he had to leave the city the next morning to meet and escort him into the city. The Revenue Commissioner ranks next to the Governor, and all the mandarins have to go out to welcome him. The result of my reminder was a hurried visit very late in the evening from one of the officers who was to accompany us. He had not been told to get ready, and consequently was the bearer of a second message requesting me to wait yet another day. After some argument I was obliged again to submit, more especially as an opposite course would put my visitor to great inconvenience, and, as he was a vigorous and intelligent man, it was important to secure his goodwill for the journey. Another person came to see me about the same time, who had been to Bhamo, and was able to say a good deal about the road to Yung-ch'ang Fu, which will be of use to me. He had some official capacity in his expedition to Bhamo, and was well acquainted with Mr. Cooper, our political agent at the town, whose card he produced. A lithograph portrait of the King of Burmah, (after a sketch by Col. Yule) was in his possession, and he seemed extremely delighted to have such a treasure. The Viceroy was to see it when he had an audience. He told me that the tribes inhabiting the country between Bhamo and Yün Nan were dreadful robbers, and that travellers incurred heavy mulcts at every town on the road.

December 1st.—This morning I had a visit from the other official who was to accompany us. He was a middle-aged man with a very dark visage, well tanned by military service and exposure. This grim warrior had an agreeable manner and a kindly disposition, and I felt well satisfied with both my conductors. They are named Chou and Yang, respectively. Both of them, civilian and soldier, were engaged in the campaigns against the Mahomedans, and the taking of Ta-li Fu, and they described the rebels as fighting with great ferocity; even the wounded lying on the field being actuated with a hatred that fought to the last without seeking quarter.

December 2nd.—After the usual delay of a start, when at length everything was ready, and the pack-horses had received their loads, down came a message from Mr. Chou, begging me to wait a little for him; accordingly I despatched my baggage and servants ahead, and waited behind a full hour until it was so late that I was obliged to start, leaving a message to indicate our rendezvous for tiffin. The road passed across the valley towards the hills. Peasants were hard at work irrigating the fields with water-troughs and paddles worked by the hands. The framework was from eight to ten feet long, and portable from place to place, while one man's exertions kept the paddles revolving with rapidity, by means of bars fitted to two cranks, and held one in each hand. Several strings of animals came along the road, loaded with salt for the capital, and irritated the chairbearers greatly by their erratic motion, which continually threatened a collision with the chair. " *Chao-hu shêng-k'ou,*" "look to your animals," was the frequent cry of the bearers, followed by thwacks, which raised the ire of the apathetic muleteers and drew on a storm of choice abuse. Mules, donkeys and ponies were mixed up together in each gang, and a couple of mules invariably led the way, decorated in the most fantastic manner about the head with red rosettes and tassels surmounted with a bunch of long feathers like a Red Indian chief. I was surprised to see in one instance that the leading animals were adorned with pendants of rich brown fur, fit for a lady's boa. At 20 li we stopped for tiffin, and Chou *ta-lao-yeh* came up with us, Yang *lao-yeh* having already arrived. Chinese officials have certain progressive designations in common parlance, such as Lao-yeh, "Honourable," Ta-lao-yeh "Right Hon." and Ta-jin "Excellency," which fitly mark their rank, and afford a graceful mode of address, which has no equivalent in translation. I have been promoted *nolens volens* to the highest of these grades and treated with extraordinary respect both by my servants and chairbearers, and by the accompanying mandarins. I presume the former act on the principle that the higher they lift me the more honour they reflect on themselves. After all these delays it was hopeless to think of going 70 li, more especially as the bearers cannot fall into their stride for a day or two, and require more rest at the beginning of a journey. We consequently came to a full stop comparatively early in the afternoon at the top of a small pass between 30 and 40 li from the capital, called Pi-chi K'ou, where there was scarcely room for so large a party.

There was only one decent inn to be found, which consisted of a single large chamber, a small corner of which was boxed off with clean woodwork for superior guests. Two gaunt buffaloes were stabled in close proximity on a floor of slush; the kitchen filled a third corner, and Messrs. Chou, Yang, and three or four of our servants found their roosts along the other sides. Chou filled up the time by smoking opium. There is something attractive in the process of taking opium, which must compensate a Chinaman for a great deal of discomfort. His bedding, which merely consists of a couple of quilts, is neatly arranged by his servant, part as couch and part as pillow, and he throws himself down to play with his pipe, and tray full of inviting nicknacks, (treasures in themselves), careless of surrounding circumstances. And each whiff costs him some pleasant exertion, for fully ten minutes elapse before the pinch of opium is reduced to the proper consistency by being twisted and twirled about at the end of a short spit in the opium lamp. I had a long conversation at night with the two officers on the subject of railways, and modern inventions. They praised up the English with a flattery that I was obliged to rebuke. But their appreciation of our moderation in war was genuine, and the name of Queen Victoria was mentioned in terms of respect and admiration. They knew the history of Her Majesty's accession and reign, and the exalted character of our sovereign reflected most favourably on the estimation in which they held the nation, and its representatives in China.

December 3rd.—We only accomplished 40 li to-day, stopping at An-ning Chou. Since the war brought ruin on every town, there has not been sufficient time for resuscitation, and consequently travellers cannot move beyond stated distances where inns are to be found. To-morrow we shall have to go 70 li before a resting place can be met with, a distance which was beyond our reach to-day, and we have to remain content with the short stage. The country to-day showed signs of past cultivation, but now lies utterly deserted. A large quantity of young trees grew on the hill sides, and we were not far from a range of mountains. The hedgerows and surrounding ground abounded with brambles, and the cactus appeared in thick bushes. The road was still full of carriers occupied with nothing else but salt. Even oxen were in requisition, saddled with packs like the ponies, and they lumbered along over the roughly-paved track with great difficulty. The coolies here do not use the bamboo much. They carry a truck on the back, which is hooked over the shoulders and curves forward above the head. Upon this they fix their load, and a very heavy one it often appears to be. Numbers of women with stout bare legs carried tremendous bundles of fuel in baskets fastened in a similar way over their shoulders. Many instances of the goitre complaint have now begun to appear among the peasants. The Chinese attribute the existence of this malady, so common among mountaineers, to some deleterious quality of the salt in general use, and I was amused one day by my servant seriously warning me not to eat it. At An-ning Chou, I was paid extraordinary honours by the local authorities. The Viceroy has most certainly kept his word with regard to notifying the mandarins en route of my approach, for the Sub-Prefect and Deputy went out to meet me in full dress, and actually knelt when I left my chair to acknowledge the compliment. Few words passed, as they begged me to be seated and shouted out "to the Yamên." I arrived before my hosts, and seemed to be installed, as though I were a Chinese superior, master of the establishment, for the mandarins sent in their cards, and in their own Yamên humbly asked if I would see them. Throughout the interview they observed the rigid etiquette of inferiors, while I was forced to play the part of a real mandarin of authority, much to my inward amusement. It was a poor house, for a new official residence had not yet been built; I was put into the best room, one which the Viceroy himself had occupied. It was just eight feet by six. Our host further honoured us by having a big dinner prepared, to which I sat down in company with my two good protectors and the writer. I saw no more of the Sub-Prefect till next morning, when he came out to pay his respects before we departed. The city walls were completely destroyed and nothing had been done yet to rebuild them. A couple of hundred houses constitute the city at present.

December 4th.—Having a long stage before us, we started early. The thermometer marked 46°, and a thick white mist filled the air, until the sun rose high enough to dispel it; and the rest of the day was almost uncomfortably hot. The road was rough and deeply indented by mule tracks. Hundreds of animals met us, employed in carrying salt. The narrowness of the track, and the undulating nature of the ground, made it extremely difficult to pass them without a collision. The chair-bearers did not hesitate to strike the muleteers as well as their beasts, and I was surprised at the meekness with which the blows were received. The Chinese lower orders are apt to be high-handed when they serve officials, but I forbade my men to touch the drivers again, however provoking their stupidity, lest they should lay at the door of the foreigner the cause of such rough treatment. The greater part of the way was waste, uncultivable land covered with hardy shrubs and stunted trees. But now and then a valley appeared which was partially retilled, and one or two villages, re-established among ruins, stood prettily embowered among trees. The semicivilised border tribes seem to trade occasionally in the province, for we passed a group to-day with their ponies carrying salt. They seldom come below Ta-li Fu. But these probably finding employment for their animals thought it worth while to go further. They wore coloured, embroidered garments and presented other peculiarities which I had not time to notice in passing. While halting to rest at a tea-shop, my men began to discuss the manners and customs of these "barbarians." They do not pass the night in the villages, but camp out on the hills, and the chief accomplishment they possess, according to my interlocutors, is to bring down birds on the wing with their arrows in such a manner as to make them fall close beside them. On arriving at the town of Lao-ya Kuan, we had to put up at a wonderful specimen of an inn. There was plenty of accommodation for animals and drivers, but only one or two small rooms for guests. I found one good room, however, and took possession thereof. We met at this place a messenger sent from the next city by the Magistrate to attend to our wants and provide anything that was required. It appears that the orders of the Viceroy have been stringent and liberal. Each official along the road has been instructed to supply horses and bearers if necessary. It so happens that my writer sustained some injury to-day by a severe fall from his pony, and my conductors have ordered the Magistrate's messenger to procure a mountain chair and two bearers for him to-morrow. They all tell me it is my duty to make some requisitions or else both I and my retinue will "lose face," as they term it.

December 5th.—On rising I was informed that the Magistrate had sent down his cook as well, and that breakfast was provided for the whole party. And a very good breakfast it proved to be. There was one excellent circular dish containing duck, fowl and pork, with vegetables swimming in a substratum of broth very much after the manner of an *à la blaize* pan. The road to-day has outdone everything hitherto encountered in utter badness. In addition to its natural imperfections, I believe the retreating Mahomedans purposely destroyed the pavement in order to throw difficulties in the way of the Imperial troops. It is far from being an easy task to describe the incredible obstacles which are suffered to remain unheeded on this track. In the first place there is scarcely any level ground in the whole length of this tedious stage of 75 li to Lu-fêng Hsien. It is full of steep passes, the chief of which rises to 3,500 feet (by my aneroid), and the track by which it is surmounted is simply a chaos of deep ruts and broken stones, offering the acme of dangerous footing to animals as well as carriers. Chair-bearers have to be supplemented by six or eight coolies dragging a rope passed round the chair, and even with this aid it is difficult to conceive how they retain their footing at the rate they press up the incline. Often it appears to be only a feat of balancing skill which saves a dangerous fall, and many are the knocks sustained by the traveller from the collisions between his chair and projecting stones. In many places the steep path has a horizontal slope as well, and to complicate the danger, pack animals passing both ways have to be avoided. At one point in this wretched highway I was saved from an imminent collapse by the strength and marvellous stability of the four bearers. There was a stampede of loose animals trying to press by us in a narrow place just as a string of loaded mules arrived from the opposite direction. The result of which was that the rope pullers got entangled and thrown over, dragging the chair aside in their fall. The usual babel of altercation followed, and the ragged tracker, who was most hurt by the fall, seized the head drover, without resistance on his part, neither of them indeed shewing any signs of exasperation whatever. It was curious to see a big strapping man like the drover, who wore good clothes, quietly submitting to be clawed and detained by a miserable starveling in rags. But it was the dread of officialdom which affected him, for he knelt down in his confusion to my official messenger, who quickly released him, and the coolie only got laughed at by his companions for his pains. On arriving at Lu-fêng Hsien, I was greeted outside the city by the Magistrate's card bearer who knelt according to custom, holding up his master's card, and politely informed me that the official travelling quarters were ready for my reception. Messrs. Chou and Yang invariably pass on ahead to prepare everything before my arrival, and I found them at the door as usual, ready to receive me. We were soon comfortably installed in two side-rooms, and dinner was served from the Magistrate's kitchen in the centre compartment. Having sent my card with polite excuses for not visiting the Magistrate at so late an hour, I was pleased to receive a visit from him later without ceremony. He was a Ssŭ-ch'uan man, Hsiao by name, and like all his fellow provincials exceedingly intelligent and agreeable. The city was still in ruins and only contained a small number of houses.

December 6th.—We started after doing justice to the Magistrate's breakfast, at an early hour, in a thick white mist (which the officials one and all so much dread), and the thermometer at 46°. The stage was the longest we have yet accomplished, being 90 li, and much of it over steep passes. The mountains were thickly covered with pine. All the villages were in ruins, and the valleys, of which we crossed three or four, are sparsely inhabited. One very heavy pass involving several li of a severe incline, though fortunately without many bad places on the road, intervenes in the long march, and by a steep descent leads to the town of Shê-tzŭ, where there is an inn and a dilapidated official rest, or Kung-kuan. Messrs. Chou and Yang thought the inn preferable, but I was obliged to alter their choice, and select the Kung-kuan for my bed. The place was quite empty and I was obliged to request the Pa-tsung, or Ensign, who had charged of the town, to supply me with tables and chairs, which he readily did. My servants spread their quilts on straw, and we got through the night fairly well, considering it was bitterly cold. It is surprising how the Chinese neglect good property. This Kung-kuan, and all others, were repaired and cleaned only last year for the Governor; but as soon as he had passed, not a soul was left in charge, and the paper ceiling has all but come down, while the walls have become begrimed with dirt and smoke from impromptu fires lighted by vagabonds on the floor. Yet it was preferable to the inn. Messrs. Chou and Yang thought they had offended me by having chosen the latter, but I soon reassured them over some mulled claret. Chou is a young man and as affected as some women are; full of mannerism, and pointing his conversation with histrionic movements of eyes, lips and brow. Yang on the other hand is an honest blunt soldier, hale and hearty under the weight of 65 years with a deep voice and kindly eye. His face is so dark that he looks like a mechanic, while blackened teeth and rough hands bear out the impression. He takes great care of me and exerts himself far more than the other. I remarked with satisfaction to-day that the road of the salt carriers branched away from ours. I hope to add some remarks about the salt trade when I have made further inquiries. On entering and leaving Sai-tsŭ, I was saluted by half a dozen of the Pa-tsung's soldiers, who prostrated themselves to perform the k'o-t'ou, and shouted out the usual formula of welcome or good speed.

December 7th.— The temperature was 42° at starting, but before very long the sun shone out strong, and by sunset the thermometer had risen 20 degrees. The difficulty of dressing in accordance with the weather becomes a hardship under such circumstances. The road was still full of difficult passes and deserted villages, and one could not help deploring the existence of such barriers to the advance of commerce. If only an easy road lay ready between Yun Nan Fu and Bhamo a perfect flood of British goods would be swallowed up at once for the Kwei Chou and Ssŭ Ch'uan markets. The merchants of the latter province would naturally prefer to buy at Yun Nan, and float their goods down the Yang-tzŭ, to the risk and expense of the difficult ascent from Hankow up the I-ch'ang gorge. Native cloth is so dear in Kwei Chou and Yun Nan, that the people cannot afford to buy it, and their ragged appearance is due not so much to poverty as to the price of cloth being beyond their means. There would be an immense sale if only Manchester goods could be cheaply conveyed. Matches have not penetrated so far, and the people envy me the possession of them. Watches are wanted badly by the rich classes. And there is a great eagerness to know the price of most of my foreign productions. Cutlery and ordinary crockery excite admiration, and almost anything foreign would speedily entice buyers if I may judge by the high appreciation and unfeigned coveting displayed by the few who examined my possessions. The country on this side of Yun Nan Fu is sadly deserted. We lunched to-day on the brow of a hill in the open air. A woman held a stall on the spot and sold rice and other food. We lighted bush fires and eat in picnic style, seated on logs of timber brought up for building purposes and undergoing preparation then and there in the hands of carpenters. The latter use similar tools to those employed by our workmen, but they apply the axe in many operations where saw and plane would ensure more finished work. Kuang-t'ung Hsien, our destination, lay in a fine valley which sadly wanted inhabitants to recultivate its broad acres. I was exceedingly well received by the Magistrate who was a young Kwei Chou man, and before leaving we became great friends. His jurisdiction was a very poor one for want of men and habitations, nor was the Yamên a fit house for his own residence. Yet everything in it showed taste and liberality, and although he had but three habitable rooms he managed to make me and my three "gentlemen" (viz. writer and two Wei-yuans) thoroughly comfortable. He gave us an excellent dinner and equally good break-fast. This part of his hospitality was however due to the acting Viceroy's orders, which I am privately informed instruct every official en route to expend six tacls on my entertainment and requirements. The rope pullers and extra coolies are all supplied by the local authorities, and I am sorry to say at little expense, for there is a class of men and boys who are constantly called out for this mandarin service and receive scarcely sufficient rumuneration to buy them rice. I created extraordinary surprise and admiration in the breasts of my six diminutive traekers by the present of 100 cash each, or in this local currency the equivalent of $3\frac{1}{2}$d. They never get a cash from mandarins after toiling like slaves over the high passes. I shall have to add some remarks on their condition.

December 8th.—The temperature was exceptionally high this morning (58°.) and the sun raised it to 66°. by 2 p.m. The whole day has been clear and warm, in spite of a southerly wind. We left Kuang-t'ung highly pleased with our reception. It is amusing how all my servants share the honours paid to me and plume themselves in the reflected rays. They even tell me so, and acknowledge my bounty with thanks, as if I commanded all this attention of my own inception. The Magistrate both welcomed and dismissed us with the usual salute of three loud crackers. The road was far better to-day and only two insignificant passes had to be crossed; but there were still some impracticable spots with footing only fit for mules. From a tourist's point of view the scenery was rather pretty. Young trees covered the hills and shaded the road in many of its windings. There were more villages and peasants and we crossed several good valleys. The last of these in the long stage was of a wide extent and full of ruins. The houses here are built partly of sun-dried mud bricks in large squares, and partly of massive walls of the same material piled up like similar structures in "concrete" elsewhere. These walls evidently resisted destruction, for they stand in silent attestation of ruin all around, and frequently deceive one with the appearance of extant villages. I lunched at a town called Yao-chan, which lies in a fine valley watered by a good-sized stream, and contains some inns. The road followed the banks of this river for the latter half of the stage almost up to the prefectural city of Ch'u-hsiung where we stopped. Some peasants were engaged in floating timber down the stream. It was all cut into small lengths, and myriads of these covered the face of the river, part in swift motion with the main current, and part lazily floating down the sluggish flow, while a quantity remained jambed in an immovable mass. The wood-cutters running along the banks with poles seemed to have no easy task in hand to keep their straggling property together. The villagers appeared to be better off and more comfortably clad in the Ch'u-hsiung district. Those of them who hailed from Yung-ch'ang Fu or T'êng-yueh Chou on the borders showed a decided predilection for colour and embroidery about their persons. Several individuals wore scarlet jackets of a ribbed cloth which I am told is a product of T'êng-yueh Chou, and I noticed how many of the wayfarers who met us on the road were becomingly decked with waist-bands or cummerbunds of pale pink or yellow. This taste for colour is no doubt derived from the example of their nomadic neighbours on the borders of Yun Nan, and presents a very agreeable contrast to the uniform dark blue which otherwise prevails throughout China as the national dress. A shopman who was clothed in the red jacket above mentioned told me that the price of the material at T'êng-yueh was Tls. 2.5 per ten feet (Chinese) and on my asking the width he held out his hands three or four feet apart saying it was of a good broad measure.

On descending the last pass the city of Ch'u-hsiung came in full

48

view at some distance across the splendid valley, situated under the hills toward the southern boundary of the plain. Once on level ground and with the goal in view, my chair-bearers and rope pullers set off at a run, with encouraging shouts and frolicsome laughter, until they ran against a bank and fairly upset me on my side. After this catastrophe a becoming gravity suddenly replaced their mirth mingled with fear for having so offended the Ta-jên. But I had suffered too many falls to care about one more, and soon after we met the Magistrate's messenger who as usual came to bid me welcome from the Yamên. The city walls enclosed an almost houseless waste. Only the high street, together with a few houses which had crystallized in its neighbourhood, had as yet arisen out of the ashes. The Prefect was living in a temple converted temporarily into his Yamên, and the Hsien occupied side quarters in the same building. I called on both, although the lateness of the hour required torches. Neither received me. This apparent incivility, from an English point of view, was really a mark of respect; for in Chinese etiquette the refusal is meant to convey a sense of inferiority, and unworthiness to accept the honour of a visit. On my return to the inn, which had been cleared out and prepared for my reception in the want of any official building for the purpose, the Prefect, who was unwell, sent his card, and the Magistrate called in person just as I and my bear-leaders were sitting down to the dinner provided by him. After the necessary bowing and preliminary civilities we resumed our chop-sticks at the request of our host who sat down alongside and kept up a sparkling conversation about Shanghai, and the splendid steamers on the river. He thought the roast mutton served on board these palaces at dinner, time was excellent, and after exhausting his eulogy of foreign manufactures, gracefully withdrew and left us to finish our meal. He was a tall, clean, well-dressed man, with an almost European face and engaging manners. Ssŭ Ch'uan again deserved my thorough appreciation of her sons.

December 9th.—We started early this morning in order to accomplish a very long stage. The proper resting place was in a village, but as the road was said to be level we determined to break into the next day's march in order to reach the city of Chên-nan Chou, and so avoid the discomforts of a country lodging. The men were persuaded to go the extra 30 li, and no doubt the good things of a Yamên added their enticement to make them undergo 95 li. In so long a march the phases of country naturally varied considerably. The road was certainly good, not however without exceptions, and the bearers were able to keep up a fast pace throughout. After passing through the rich valley of Ch'u-hsiung Fu, we crossed a series of low easy passes, always leading to a valley, with the surrounding hills prettily covered with young pine trees. The country was less and less inhabited as we proceeded, and the people more miserably clothed; often wide flats appeared, given up to rank grass, and occasionally the road crossed a desert of brambles and wild bushes growing on a hard bed of clay. There was a quantity of pure white clay fit for porcelain, and different coloured mounds of Lias gave a strange aspect to the ground. Coal cropped out at one spot, and a shaft was actually being worked higher up on the hill. Buffalo carts reappeared on the plains, and a river frequently had to be crossed over good stone bridges. In the earlier part of the stage a good deal of building was being carried on by rich proprietors, and I noticed one example of the way they construct the massive earth walls so characteristic of the district round about. The mud was thrown in between planks of wood, and battened down with clubs. Each layer became hardened in the sun, and the wall had the appearance of being built in strata of about a foot thick. An amusing incident occurred on leaving Ch'u-hsiung Fu. Just as we passed the door of the Yamên, a miserable looking dog which had lost almost the last shreds of his coat through mange, placed itself at the head of my procession, and persistently escorted us for 60 li. He rested where we rested, and never failed to pick out my chair from among the others as the special object of his care. I set the whole crowd of Chinamen in a roar of laughter by suggesting that this must be the Chih-hsien's especial messenger sent to escort me. On reaching Chên-nan Chou we were very comfortably installed in the Yamên, which was in a better condition than most. The Sub-Prefect was away in the country, but he returned at night, and came in to see me after dinner. He was a quiet, agreeable man of somewhat over 50, and a native of Shan-Tung. His cook must have followed him from the north judging by the superiority of his culinary skill over all the other cooks who had regaled us hitherto. There was a good deal of traffic on the road, but it consisted of the cheapest and most ordinary objects of daily use, such as pottery, calibashes, hats and straw shoes. The high street, in the cities, was always full of stalls, most of which displayed native cloth for sale in small quantities.

December 10th.—Having cut out 30 li of to-day's stage, and the country ahead being thinly populated, we could not go beyond the regular resting place, which was now only 35 li distant. Accordingly the whole party gladly availed themselves of half a day's rest in comfortable quarters. I wrote my letters till 1 P.M., and then, after a short interview with our worthy host, took my departure for the town of Sha-ch'iao. The Sub-Prefect gave us a good breakfast, and sent on his cook and servant to prepare dinner for us at the next stage where there was no Yamên. He was also good enough to present me with a live goat which is destined to feed us during the next four stages, traversing a mountainous district wherein no city is to be met with, and we shall I presume be thrown on our own resources at small country towns. The road to-day crossed one or two hills, and then descended into a beautiful valley well cultivated and containing many villages. The town of Sha-ch'iao came in view about two miles away and covered a large extent of ground. On entering it we observed that the place had suffered less in the war than its neighbours, and can now compare favourably with the walled cities in size and population. I could not judge fairly of the latter, however, as it was market day and the main street was thronged with country folk. We were lodged in a remarbably good Kung-kuan which showed signs of having been a temple once. With a clear sky and hot sun, the temperature was uncomfortably high all day. There was a strong breeze blowing from the north, towards sunset, but we fortunately escaped its attendant dust by a speedy arrival at our resting place.

December 11th.—We had to rise early this morning as 95 li lay between us and the next resting place, a town called P'ù-p'êng by the natives, but which is entered in the Chinese map as Lien-p'êng. The first 30 li of the way skirted the well cultivated valley of Sha-ch'iao, where we rested last night, and the road thus far was level and really good. Then followed 20 li of steep climbing up a narrow ravine, which was full of trees and shrubs, and contained a brook of clear mountain water tumbling down at a great velocity. It was a beautiful piece of natural scenery, but the dangers of the rough and tortuous track, by which we had to thread our way marred the pleasure which it excited. It was disturbing to be hung over a precipice at an angle of about 30°, while the bearers were turning a sharp corner, and to feel the slips which they could scarcely avoid on the loose red sand which thinly covered the rock underfoot. It was one long ascent every inch of the way, until we reached a village at the summit, which was the halfway rest. It was a poor place and could not afford a decent lodging for a European traveller. He must go 45 li further for that. The remainder of the road was tolerably good. It first descended a ravine slightly, and then followed a high level over-hanging a deep precipice well veiled with trees. This debouched at length on to an arid uncultivable plateau of red sandstone, undulating, and sparsely covered with shrubs and a few stunted trees. Along this desert we were on a level with the tops of a mass of hills stretching away before us as far as the eye could see. A little cultivation was carried on in terraces, but otherwise it seemed to be a red sand waste far and wide. I was surprised to see quite a large town in the midst of this wild plateau, and still more to find that it contained a Yamèn, in which we were soon very comfortably settled and fed by the hospitality of the Prefect of Yao-chou, in whose jurisdiction the town lay, and who had actually sent down his servants a distance of 180 li, or two day's journey, from the city to provide for us. Such incomparable civility proves how thoroughly the Viceroy is to be relied on. His career has been marked by "thoroughness." I listen daily to stories of his remarkable campaigns against the Miautsze in Kuei Chou, and the Mahomedans in Yun Nan, which the old soldier Yang loves to dilate upon after dinner. But as his accent is provokingly provincial, I unfortunately cannot keep pace with his rapid utterance, but I hope to know all about this hero before returning to Yun-nan Fu where I have been promised the honour of an interview. The Ta-li Fu people are trouble-some and dangerous. I was told so by the Chên-nan Magistrate, and it was for this reason that the Viceroy sent two mandarins with me. We are four stages from that city, and I am to remain a whole day at the previous stage, while Chou and Yang go ahead to ensure arrange-ments for my comfort and safety.

For EU product safety concerns, contact us at Calle de José Abascal, 56–1°, 28003 Madrid, Spain or eugpsr@cambridge.org.

www.ingramcontent.com/pod-product-compliance
Ingram Content Group UK Ltd.
Pitfield, Milton Keynes, MK11 3LW, UK
UKHW012336130625
459647UK00009B/312